The International Organization for Standardization (ISO)

The International Organization for Standardization (ISO) is the first full-length study of the largest non-governmental, global regulatory network whose scope and influence rivals that of the UN system.

Much of the interest in the successes and failures of global governance focuses around high-profile organizations such as the United Nations, World Bank, and World Trade Organization. This volume is one of few books that explore both the International Organization for Standardization's (ISO) role as a facilitator of essential economic infrastructure and the implication of ISO techniques for a much wider realm of global governance.

Through detailing the initial rationale behind the ISO and a systematic discussion of how this low-profile organization has developed, the authors provide a comprehensive survey of the ISO as a powerful force in the way commerce is conducted in a changing and increasingly globalized world.

Craig N. Murphy is M. Margaret Ball Professor of International Relations at Wellesley College. He is past president of the International Studies Association, past chair of the Academic Council on the UN System, and a founding editor of the international public policy journal *Global Governance.*

JoAnne Yates is Sloan Distinguished Professor of Management and Deputy Dean at MIT's Sloan School of Management. Her research encompasses both historical and contemporary organizations with a focus on changing communication and information technologies and the related work practices.

Routledge Global Institutions

Edited by Thomas G. Weiss
The CUNY Graduate Center, New York, USA
and Rorden Wilkinson
University of Manchester, UK

About the Series

The Global Institutions Series is designed to provide readers with comprehensive, accessible, and informative guides to the history, structure, and activities of key international organizations. Every volume stands on its own as a thorough and insightful treatment of a particular topic, but the series as a whole contributes to a coherent and complementary portrait of the phenomenon of global institutions at the dawn of the millennium.

Books are written by recognized experts, conform to a similar structure, and cover a range of themes and debates common to the series. These areas of shared concern include the general purpose and rationale for organizations, developments over time, membership, structure, decision-making procedures, and key functions. Moreover, current debates are placed in historical perspective alongside informed analysis and critique. Each book also contains an annotated bibliography and guide to electronic information as well as any annexes appropriate to the subject matter at hand.

The volumes currently published or under contract include:

The United Nations and Human Rights (2005)
A guide for a new era
by Julie Mertus (American University)

The UN Secretary General and Secretariat (2005)
by Leon Gordenker (Princeton University)

United Nations Global Conferences (2005)
by Michael G. Schechter (Michigan State University)

The UN General Assembly (2005)
by M.J. Peterson (University of Massachusetts, Amherst)

Internal Displacement (2006)
Conceptualization and its consequences
by Thomas G. Weiss (The CUNY Graduate Center) and David A. Korn

Global Environmental Institutions (2006)
by Elizabeth R. DeSombre (Wellesley College)

African Economic Institutions
by Kwame Akonor (Seton Hall University)

The United Nations Development Programme (UNDP)
by Elizabeth A. Mandeville (Tufts University) and Craig N. Murphy (Wellesley College)

The Regional Development Banks
Lending with a regional flavor
by Jonathan R. Strand (University of Nevada, Las Vegas)

Multilateral Cooperation Against Terrorism
by Peter Romaniuk (John Jay College of Criminal Justice, CUNY)

Peacebuilding
From concept to commission
by Robert Jenkins (University of London)

Transnational Organized Crime
by Frank Madsen (University of Cambridge)

Governing Climate Change
by Peter Newell (University of East Anglia) and Harriet A. Bulkeley (Durham University)

Millennium Development Goals (MDGs)
For a people-centered development agenda?
by Sakiko Fukada-Parr (The New School)

Regional Security
The capacity of international organizations
by Rodrigo Tavares (United Nations University)

Human Development
by Maggie Black

Human Security
by Don Hubert (University of Ottawa)

Global Poverty
by David Hulme (University of Manchester)

UNICEF
by Richard Jolly (University of Sussex)

UNESCO
by J.P. Singh (Georgetown University)

For further information regarding the series, please contact:

Craig Fowlie, Publisher, Politics & International Studies
Taylor & Francis
2 Park Square, Milton Park, Abingdon
Oxford OX14 4RN, UK

+44 (0)207 842 2057 Tel
+44 (0)207 842 2302 Fax

Craig.Fowlie@tandf.co.uk
www.routledge.com

The International Organization for Standardization (ISO)

Global governance through voluntary consensus

Craig N. Murphy and JoAnne Yates

Routledge
Taylor & Francis Group

LONDON AND NEW YORK

First published 2009
by Routledge
2 Park Square, Milton Park, Abingdon, Oxon, OX14 4RN

Simultaneously published in the USA and Canada
by Routledge
711 Third Avenue, New York, NY 10017

Routledge is an imprint of the Taylor & Francis Group, an informa business

Typeset in Times New Roman by
Taylor & Francis Books

British Library Cataloguing in Publication Data
A catalogue record for this book is available from the British Library

Library of Congress Cataloging in Publication Data
Murphy, Craig.
    The International Organization for Standardization (ISO) : global
governance through voluntary consensus / Craig N. Murphy and
JoAnne Yates.
        p. cm. – (Global institutions)
    Includes bibliographical references and index.
    1. Standardization. 2. International Organization for Standardization.
    3. Corporate governance. 4. Industrialization–International
    cooperation. I. Yates, JoAnne, 1951- II. Title.
    HD62.M77 2008
389'.60601–dc22   2008028346

ISBN 978-0-415-77429-1 (hbk)
ISBN 978-0-415-77428-4 (pbk)
ISBN 978-0-203-88434-8 (ebk)

Contents

Illustrations

Figures

Tables

Boxes

Foreword

The current volume is the thirty-second in a dynamic series on "global institutions." The series strives (and, based on the volumes published to date, succeeds) to provide readers with definitive guides to the most visible aspects of what many of us know as "global governance." Remarkable as it may seem, there exist relatively few books that offer in-depth treatments of prominent global bodies, processes, and associated issues, much less an entire series of concise and complementary volumes. Those that do exist are either out of date, inaccessible to the non-specialist reader, or seek to develop a specialized understanding of particular aspects of an institution or process rather than offer an overall account of its functioning. Similarly, existing books have often been written in highly technical language or have been crafted "in-house" and are notoriously self-serving and narrow.

The advent of electronic media has undoubtedly helped research and teaching by making data and primary documents of international organizations more widely available, but it has also complicated matters. The growing reliance on the Internet and other electronic methods of finding information about key international organizations and processes has served, ironically, to limit the educational and analytical materials to which most readers have ready access—namely, books. Public relations documents, raw data, and loosely refereed web sites do not make for intelligent analysis. Official publications compete with a vast amount of electronically available information, much of which is suspect because of its ideological or self-promoting slant. Paradoxically, a growing range of purportedly independent web sites offering analyses of the activities of particular organizations has emerged, but one inadvertent consequence has been to frustrate access to basic, authoritative, readable, critical, and well-researched texts. The market for such has actually been reduced by the ready availability of varying quality electronic materials.

For those of us who teach, research, and practice in the area, such limited access to information has been particularly frustrating. We were delighted when Routledge saw the value of a series that bucks this trend and provides key reference points to the most significant global institutions and issues. They are betting that serious students and professionals will want serious analyses. We have assembled a first-rate line-up of authors to address that market. Our intention, then, is to provide one-stop shopping for all readers—students (both undergraduate and post-graduate), negotiators, diplomats, practitioners from non-governmental and intergovernmental organizations, and interested parties alike—seeking information about the most prominent institutional aspects of global governance.

The International Organization for Standardization

Much of the interest in what we commonly know as global governance is focused on the successes and failures of the United Nations (UN) and the principal economic institutions of the International Monetary Fund (IMF),[1] World Bank,[2] and World Trade Organization (WTO).[3] This attention, however, belies a more intimate and creeping process of globalization engendered by a series of relatively unknown global institutions overseeing largely functional tasks. Indeed, we can learn much (and potentially much more) about global governance by exploring those institutions that are relatively hidden from public view but which perform tasks that governments not only agree to but which have a real impact on everyday life, than we can from their "headline" counterparts. The Bank for International Settlements (BIS), for instance, works to harmonize national and international banking systems by bringing together 55 central banks. Yet, the organization is virtually invisible and has certainly not been subject to the kind of public protests encountered by its more familiar economic counterparts—the IMF and World Bank. Similarly, the World Organization for Animal Health (the OIE—formerly the Office International des Epizooties, hence the acronym), although a key player in national and international standard setting in animal health and disease prevention and a partner organization of the WTO, does not attract the kind of attention that the World Trade Organization has "enjoyed." The same can be said of the organization that is the subject of this book: the International Organization for Standardization (ISO)—a key player in assisting the advance of industrialization as well as shaping patterns of production and consumption, but a relatively hidden institution nonetheless.

The ISO is a non-governmental institution (albeit one that was established under the aegis of the UN) bridging public and private sectors and is the self-proclaimed international standard setter for "business, government and society," through its pursuit of voluntary standards. The organization boasts having developed more than 17,000 international standards in its 60-year history and claims that it is engaged in producing an additional 1,100 standards each year. These standards range from those dealing with size, clarity, and weights of jewelry through clothing measures to the systems businesses ought to put in place to enhance customer satisfaction. Its work thus has an intimate impact on daily life by shaping and molding the way in which commerce is conducted, the operating procedures of business, and the way in which consumers engage with markets.

The story of the ISO is not, however, merely one associated with its development since its founding in 1946 (operational from 1947). It draws on a long tradition of standard setting that was crucial to the advance of industrialization in the nineteenth century. Some of this standard setting was the result of government and business agreement on product development; others were the consequence of commercial battles fought out over the most appropriate format for such items as video recorders and the like; others still were intimately connected with the spread of imperialism such as the standardization of railway gauges, the operational language of air traffic control, and the way in which we measure time (by the hour as well as by the day, week, and year).

To write this book we needed authors who intimately understood both standard setting and global governance. We knew of the perfect partnership in Craig Murphy and JoAnne Yates. Craig Murphy, currently M. Margaret Ball Professor of International Relations at Wellesley College, is a leading authority and has written extensively on global governance, including an unusual optic that begins in 1850 and not the 1990s.[4] He is one of the very few scholars to have explored in detail the connections between international institutionalization and industrialization. His recent work on standard setting is a natural extension of this work. He is author and editor of, among other things, some of the most influential books in the theory and practice of international relations,[5] including his recent masterful history of the United Nations Development Programme.[6]

JoAnne Yates, Sloan Distinguished Professor of Management at the Sloan School of Management, Massachusetts Institute of Technology, is one of the world's leading experts in communication and information technology. She is author and editor of, among other things, several of the leading texts that are widely used in business schools.[7]

We could not have found two authors better placed to write this intriguing volume. What follows is an account not only of the development of the international organization of standard setting but of the politics and political economy of commercial and state rivalry. It is a first-rate work and one that should be read by all interested in global governance. We are persuaded that readers will enjoy the volume as much for its engaging style as for its content.

As always, we look forward to comments from first-time or veteran readers of the Global Institutions series.

Thomas G. Weiss, The CUNY Graduate Center, New York, USA
Rorden Wilkinson, University of Manchester, UK
November 2008

Acknowledgments

We are grateful to Thomas G. Weiss and Rorden Wilkinson for their interest in our research and their encouragement throughout the project. The Massachusetts Institute of Technology (MIT) and Wellesley College provided us with research support, including funding the work of Maria Nassén through the MIT Undergraduate Research Opportunity Program. Craig was supported through a sabbatical year fellowship at the Radcliffe Institute for Advanced Study, which also funded two Harvard University research assistants, Naa Ammah-Tagoe and Honor McGee; we thank those institutions, our research assistants, the other Fellows at Radcliffe who were a constant source of information and inspiration, and those who wrote in support of Craig's sabbatical application: Tom, Rorden, Christopher Candland, Mark Malloch Brown, and Mark Suzman. We are grateful to all those who helped us gain access to original documents and relevant bibliographies, especially Beatrice Frey at ISO, Stacy Leistner at the American National Standards Institute, Robert C. McWilliam for help throughout the United Kingdom, Marc Levinson and Hugo van Driel for works on container transport, and Lars and Lolo Sturén for giving us access to the papers of their father, Olle Sturén. Levinson also provided us with Figure 3.1, for which we are particularly grateful.

Abbreviations

AFNOR	Association Française de Normalisation
ANAB	ANSI-ASQ National Accreditation Board
ANSI	American National Standards Institute
ASA	American Standards Association
ASQ	American Society for Quality
BBC	British Broadcasting Corporation
BIPM	Bureau International des Poids et Mesures
BSI	British Standards Institute
CASCO	Committee on Conformity Assessment
CEN	European Committee for Standardization
GATT	General Agreement on Tariffs and Trade
GMO	Genetically Modified Organism
IAF	International Accreditation Forum
ICC	Interstate Commerce Commission
IEC	International Electrotechnical Commission
IETF	Internet Engineering Task Force
ILAC	International Laboratory Accreditation Cooperation
ILO	International Labor Organization
ISA	International Federation of National Standardization Associations
ISO	International Organization for Standardization
IT	information technology
ITU	International Telecommunication Union
JISC	Japan Industrial Standards Committee
MDGs	Millennium Development Goals
MIT	Massachusetts Institute of Technology
NEN	Nederlands Normalisatie-instituut
NEDCO	Committee for the study of the Netherlands' statement concerning ISO liaisons and activities
NGO	non-governmental organization

OECD	Organization for Economic Cooperation and Development
OIML	International Organization of Legal Metrology
OSI	Open Systems Interconnection
SA	Standards Australia
SIS	Swedish Standards Institute
TC	Technical Committee
TMB	Technical Management Board
UK	United Kingdom
UN	United Nations
UNDP	United Nations Development Programme
UNSCC	United Nations Standards Coordinating Committee
USA	United States of America
W3C	World Wide Web Consortium
WHO	World Health Organization
WTO	World Trade Organization

Introduction

This book is about the International Organization for Standardization (usually just called "ISO," which is often treated as a word, not as an acronym[1]) and related organizations including its international predecessors and the International Electrotechnical Commission (IEC, founded in 1906 and considered an autonomous part of ISO since its founding in 1946) as well as the larger principle of "voluntary consensus standard setting" which all of them embody.

ISO and its predecessors began as facilitators of agreements on industrial standards, "nuts and bolts" issues, including the technical specifications of actual bolts, screws, and nuts! Such agreements provide necessary infrastructure for the increasingly global industrial economy. As one of the figures in the early twentieth-century global standards movement, Paul G. Agnew, the head of the major industrial standards body in the United States of America, put it:

> In the flow of products from farm, forest, mine, and sea through processing and fabricating plants, and through wholesale and retail markets to the ultimate consumer, most difficulties are met at the transition points—points at which the product passes from department to department within a company, or is sold by one company to another or to an individual. The main function of standards is to facilitate the flow of products through these transition points. Standards are thus both facilitators and integrators. In smoothing out points of difficulty, or "bottlenecks," they provide the evolutionary adjustments which are necessary for industry to keep pace with technical advances.[2]

Agnew believed that standard setting was key to the healthy development of industrial economies. Some admirers of standard setting made even grander claims. They argued that the voluntary consensus process that ISO and its predecessors employed could solve many difficult problems of governance, leading to improvements in health, public safety, the conditions of labor, and the like. The process uses committees composed of professional engineers, employees of government agencies, and representatives of companies that produce and companies that purchase specific products or services to come to consensus over standards that future producers can choose to adopt or reject.

Champions of the process believe that its openness, as well as its aim of achieving solutions that are "scientific" or "technical" rather than "political," assures the legitimacy of the resulting standards, and, hence, their widespread adoption. In 1920, the Fabian social theorists Sidney and Beatrice Webb wrote that it was "impossible to over-rate the importance in the control of industry of this silent but all-pervading determination of processes." They hoped for the "further development" of such organizations in "the public service."[3] Ten years later, Alfred Zimmern, the holder of the world's first chair in international politics, imagined similar processes solving many of the seemingly intractable problems of international governance faced by the failing League of Nations.[4]

This same argument has also been heard much more recently. In 2000, Harland Cleveland, past-president of the American Society of Public Administration and a dogged advocate of United Nations (UN) reform since the UN's very beginning, argued that the ISO's processes provide the germ of a consultative, "nobody-in-charge" global society that could greatly expand human freedom.[5] Two years later, the World Bank's vice president for Europe, Jean-François Rischard, published a lively book that called for solving the world's 20 most urgent global problems, from global warming to falling labor standards, by applying ISO's voluntary consensus process.[6]

ISO has, in fact, taken on some of the tasks that have proven too difficult for the League of Nations or the UN. These include environmental regulation, where the voluntary ISO standard, ISO 14000, may have had more impact than any of the UN-sponsored agreements of the 1990s), and questions of corporate responsibility for human rights (including core labor rights), where the new ISO 26000 could prove more successful than the UN-sponsored Global Compact.

This book explores both ISO's role as a facilitator of essential technical infrastructure ("this silent but all-pervading process") for the global economy and the future of ISO in a changing and increasingly globalized world.

We begin, in Chapter 1, with the emergence and early significance of this unusual social institution of voluntary consensus standard setting.

ISO was formed in 1946 by a relatively small group of key individuals—most of them engineers, the most prominent of them British and
American—who had been concerned with standard setting throughout
the first half of the century. These engineers had also played important
roles in establishing their countries' national standards bureaus and
non-governmental standards bodies as well as international bodies
including the IEC and ISO's League-era and wartime "United Nations"
(i.e. the "Allied nations") predecessors. The chapter outlines ISO's
entire history and focuses on these people and their work through the
early 1960s when the number of fields in which ISO "technical committees" (the multi-stakeholder bodies in which standards are negotiated) functioned began growing steadily, and ISO's membership
rapidly increased.

Chapter 2 focuses on ISO's operation, on how standards are set. It
identifies the whole range of actors involved in the global network of
voluntary consensus standard setting and identifies where power within
ISO tends to lie. It considers the general reasons that parties become
involved in ISO's work and explains how ISO's work is funded. Finally,
it explains how—despite the fact that ISO's standards are "voluntary"—most of them end up being enforced by market pressure or by
the ways in which national laws and intergovernmental treaties make
reference to international voluntary standards.

Chapter 3 considers the central role that ISO has played in contemporary economic globalization. ISO's standards for shipping containers assured the development of a technology that was necessary to today's
global commodity chains in almost all fields of manufacturing: today's
economy would not be possible without inexpensive transoceanic shipping
and that, in turn, depended on ISO standards.

The current wave of economic globalization encouraged ISO's slow
but steady movement into fields far removed from it original concern
with "nuts and bolts," the focus of Chapter 4. The new fields include
work processes (ISO 9000's "quality management" standards), environmental regulation (ISO 14000), and corporate social responsibility (ISO
26000).

Chapter 5 reflects on ISO's future in a world in which industrial
standards are increasingly contentious and difficult to create due to the
speed of technological innovation and the extent of the interconnec-
tions within the global economy. ISO standards played a role in the
creation of today's lead industries—they helped shape the way in which
information technology has been developed since the 1980s—but the
lengthy voluntary consensus process cannot keep up with the pace of
innovation. Governments and intergovernmental bodies have tried to

gain advantage by setting some standards more quickly than the ISO process, and many engineers who are concerned with maintaining relatively open access to new technologies, have embraced the "Open Source" movement—a new approach to intellectual property that addresses some of the issues addressed by standard setters in the past.

In the book's conclusion, we point out that ISO is likely to remain at the center of the global political economy throughout this century, but that its primary role may have shifted. ISO's work in the fields of corporate social responsibility and quality management, broadly conceived, will be joined to work in maintaining and updating standards in all established industrial fields, but the original problems that were solved by voluntary consensus standard setting—the standard's issues in the leading-edge technologies—are likely to be dealt with by other means.

1 Voluntary consensus standard setting

Why it matters and how it arose

To understand ISO's current role, and its future, it is essential to understand its past. That is the purpose of this chapter. We first consider the general roles that standard setting has played in all economies; standards both help determine with whom people trade—the boundaries of trading areas—as well as the form of technological innovation that takes place within a trading area. We then turn to the idea of voluntary consensus standard setting and the advantages that this method was perceived to have by its inventors, engineers active more than a century ago. ISO grew from the vision of the engineers, and from their work throughout the first half the last century, which is the next issue that this chapter addresses. Finally, we outline three eras in ISO's 60 years of operation, beginning with the two decades in which it established its capacity and developed its procedures. In the following two decades, until the late 1980s, ISO's work focused on helping create the current global trading area. In the last two decades, the focus has shifted to the broad area of management standards, and to forms of social regulation within the new global market that states have failed to provide.

Creating trading areas and shaping innovation

In the early part of the twentieth century, many standards enthusiasts believed that voluntary consensus standard setting could do almost anything—from combating Bolshevism to maintaining international peace.[1] Nevertheless, the most lasting arguments for standard setting relate to establishing the "technical infrastructure" for a modern economy, an infrastructure that includes, "measurement, calibration, testing, conformity assessment, certification and registration, [and] accreditation," as well as setting industrial standards.[2]

The mid-twentieth century heterodox economist, Polly Hill, used to lament that most economists ignored the importance of such infrastructure because they had little experience with *real* markets: locales where wares are on view, sellers are numerous, buyers and onlookers can enter freely, and outcomes are determined by a complex interaction of the participants rather than by the working out of some abstract principles.[3] In contrast, Hill conducted field research. She studied villages close to Kumasi, in today's Ghana, site of Africa's (and perhaps the world's) largest marketplace. She knew that Kejetia market—stretching from horizon to horizon from the center of this capital of the old Ashanti kingdom—was a consequence of *physical* infrastructure: the network of "Great Roads, the channels on which the state's coercive capacity flowed."[4] The market was also a consequence of a *technical* infrastructure that included the standard weights and measures established, according to legend, by an early king. By the twentieth century, that technical infrastructure was even manifest in a globally recognized art form: Ashanti gold weights.[5]

Until the British conquest in 1901, Ashanti was primarily an agricultural society that also traded in slaves and gold. Its large marketplaces were fewer in number, its physical infrastructure less complicated, and its standards less numerous than those of any contemporary industrial society. Nevertheless, it provides a model for any modern economy. The ends of the Ashanti roads marked the boundaries of what Polly Hill's contemporary, the economic historian and US policy maker W. W. Rostow, called an "interrelated trading area ... the optimum unit for the study of economic history ... the frame within which many of the most important national, regional, or even international problems must be placed if they are to be fully understood."[6]

Such trading areas do not arise naturally; they must be created. Thus, for example, today's global economy is linked by the regimes for civil aviation and for ocean shipping created after the Second World War and by all the interconnected equipment that allows shipping containers to move swiftly just as surely as nineteenth-century Ashanti was connected by the king's roads. Similarly, there are, today, tens of thousands of global product and service standards that provide a technical infrastructure as essential as the traditional gold weights of Kejetia market. As one historian of standard setting puts it, "Without this infrastructure, virtually nothing in our modern world would work: building, manufacturing, trade, retail, health care, education, communication, and transport would be paralysed."[7]

Infrastructure, both physical and technical, not only must be created, but it must also be maintained and protected. Those Great Roads that knit together nineteenth-century Ashanti were, "fragile ... subject to recurrent seasonal disruption and to very rapid deterioration if and when they were neglected."[8] Moreover, in 1898, after the British completed a railway from Kumasi to their own colonial capital on the coast, Ashanti's physical infrastructure became appended to the transportation system that linked Britain's imperial trading area. Three years later, a British governor imposed a new technical infrastructure, as well: yardsticks, pints, and pounds *directly* followed the flag, preceding the trade that was one of the aims of the British conquest.

Some scholars view late nineteenth-century imperialism as the outward expansion of the European, US, and Japanese trading areas that had grown as an almost inevitable consequence of capitalist industry.[9] Certainly, many forces within the industrial economy pushed in that direction, even if they did not make the outcome inevitable. There is no reason to recount all those forces here, although it may be worth recalling Marx and Engels' prescient summary of them, written in 1848: "[T]he rapid improvement of all instruments of production ... the immensely facilitated means of communication ... [t]he cheap prices of commodities are the heavy artillery with which it batters down all Chinese walls ... [and] creates a world after its own image."[10]

Such globalizing pressures encourage the "standardization of standards" across newly integrated regions. Moreover, *new* standards are constantly needed for all the new processes and new products that capitalist industry generates. Even though some economists and social commentators have worried that standardization tends to stifle innovation, this is rarely the case when standards are essential to the establishment of a communication or transportation network, a production process, or any system in which industrial products have to work together. As Paul Agnew, the early standards advocate in the United States, argued, what we now call "compatibility standards" resolve the "difficulties" that "are met at the transition points— points at which the product passes from department to department within a company, or is sold by one company to another or to an individual."[11]

Even when standards are not essential to link such systems, standards *always* shape competition and competition shapes innovation. Agnew's contemporary, Albert W. Whitney of the US National Bureau of Underwriters, used an unfortunate metaphor of the day to explain how this happens: "Variation is the active, creative, masculine force in evolution; standardization is the brooding, conservational, feminine force out of which comes the potency of the next advance."[12] A recent French standard setter, Jean-Daniel Merlet, has a less objectionable way of putting the point. He writes of a "triangular" relationship between standardization, regulation, and innovation.[13]

Effective industrial standards spur socially desirable innovation. For example, in the early 1990s, advertisements from mobile phone providers in the United States tended to emphasize the size of their proprietary networks, which used different standards, basically saying, "If you sign up with us, you are more likely to be able to talk to the people you want to reach." Now that the number of communication standards that link networks have been reduced, and most new phones are designed to operate using more than one standard, the same providers tend to compete on price, on innovations in their equipment, and on the services they provide[14]—hence, the iPhone and its many competitors. In Europe and Japan, and even in Africa and South Asia, where mobile phone standards were set much earlier, this competition began much earlier. In 2007, Indian teenagers were surprised to learn from a US reporter that phones in her country did not include FM radios and only a few could play downloaded movies or music.[15]

Nonetheless, despite such examples, Jean-Daniel Merlet and most other standard setters agree that some standards have come too early, and have inhibited what might have been socially valuable innovation. Similarly, some standards have come too late and have little impact on a market that is heavily invested in well established, but incompatible products or systems. However, new standards in a related field can sometimes undo the latter kind of damage. For example, anyone who uses electronic devices is familiar with the jumble of plug-in charging cables needed for our MP3 players, cameras, computers, and mobiles. Today, electronics companies actually engage in a lot of "innovation" to make those adaptors *incompatible* from product to product and even from one generation of the same product to the next; unfortunately, there is profit to be made on those cheap, relatively low-tech devices. The technology exists to have universal "charging pads" for all such devices; we would just have to place any gadgets on one pad that would plug into the wall and then the pad would send power to the battery through the air. Large-scale investment in that technology awaits a standard for transferring power via inductive coupling. If and when that standard appears, electronics manufacturers will have to look for other sources of profit, which may encourage a more fruitful kind of innovation.[16]

The power of voluntary consensus mechanisms

Everyone has faced the frustration of having products not work well, or not work well together, because no standard exists. Many of us, perhaps most of us, have had the thought: "Why don't they just make all those #@%! things the same? There really ought to be a law!"

There are, however, some good reasons for not having most standards set by law, no matter how frustrating the consequences may be. For one thing, there are too many things to legislate. Most professional estimates agree that the minimum number of standards needed in any industrial economy is in the tens of thousands.[17] Hundreds of new standards are needed each year and each standard needs to be updated constantly. As a result, when legislatures *do* set industrial standards, they have a tendency to leave them in place for decades or even generations, and inflexible, unamendable standards really *can* stifle innovation.[18]

For the most part, though, this problem never has to be faced because national governments have little interest in taking on the task. In part, this is because *local* political leaders or local monopolists often have a vested interest in maintaining traditional standards that give the local powers some significant advantage. In fact, one of the demands that fueled the French Revolution was for a single national set of weights and measures that would abolish the "seigneurage"[19] reaped by the local nobility (the *seigneurs*) who maintained incompatible standards from one district to the next, but even the great rationalist Diderot doubted that it would be possible to enforce a national system.[20] Similarly, the constitution of the first state to be founded on Enlightenment principles granted the United States Congress the right to set standards, and in President Washington's first address to the new legislature he demanded that the body take up the task. Nevertheless, another century had passed before it established an Office of Construction of Weights and Measures. In the interim, Congress delegated the task of promoting uniform weights and measures to the Treasury Department, which proved ineffective.[21] At the end of the nineteenth century, 25 different fundamental units of length were in use in the USA "[T]hree had the same length but different names, the remainder different names and values that were unrelated to each other."[22]

The situation was little different anywhere else in the world. In fact, it is possible that, immediately before the British conquest of Ashanti in 1901, the Ashanti king's fundamental standards applied over as wide a trading area as any others in the world simply because his troops *could* control what went on in the trading area's one massive marketplace.

The problem with government-set standards is not just that, before the twentieth century, governments rarely had the power to enforce even "fundamental" standards (weights and measures) over a wide territory. It is also that *representative* governments may not be interested in *exercising* the power, even if they have it. This lack of interest was the primary reason for the US Congress's inaction throughout the nineteenth century and more recently, when the latest of the periodic attempts by Congress to impose the metric system ended with Ronald Reagan's abolition of the office that was to enforce the 1975 law.[23] When legislatures set standards, they often create some costs or take away some advantage from some deeply committed constituency, which will do all it can to block legislation or enforcement. For that reason, one political scientist, reflecting on the long history of governmental standard setting, notes that, "public actors may impede standardization even in the face of high private demand and clear public welfare gains." Therefore, to understand those cases when governments have been effective standard setters, we have to understand what was in it for them, i.e. the unusual "incentives for political entrepreneurs to agree on common standards."[24]

On the other hand, many private actors—consumers, companies that produce and use different industrial goods, engineers who design them, and scientists whose work informs the engineers—often experience much stronger incentives to agree on common standards. That is why, for more than a century, non-governmental organizations (NGOs) have maintained a host of voluntary consensus standard setting mechanisms. The literature tends to lump these mechanisms together, categorizing them as standardization by "committee" (in contrast to standardization by "government" or by the long-term operation of the market). In an important article, Joseph Farrell and Garth Saloner develop formal models of standard setting under the different mechanisms.[25] Under the reasonable assumptions that Farrell and Saloner make, the kind of technical committees that exist in ISO and other voluntary consensus standard setting bodies appear superior: They actually achieve the outcome of setting a single standard and, even if significant value is placed on speed—and such committees are rarely speedy—committees still outperform the market. Typically, the market, operating alone, will result in competing standards for a relatively long period—for example, the situation that obtained for more than a decade with the competing VHS and Betamax standards for videotape or, more recently, with the competing Blu-ray versus HD DVD standards for the latest generation of video recordings.[26]

Nonetheless, Farrell and Saloner point to a mechanism that is even more effective: standard setting by committees in a world in which powerful actors (dominant firms, leading states, or formally organized trading regions such as the European Union) can defect from the process and set a standard that many others are likely to follow. This is, of course, a fairly accurate description of the world in which we actually live, a world of widespread voluntary consensus standard setting, which, by its very nature, allows powerful organizations to have the option of setting their own standards before consensus has been reached.

ISO, the standards movement, and earlier innovations in voluntary consensus standard setting

ISO is the organization at the center of a vast global network of voluntary consensus standard setting bodies that began to emerge in the second half of the nineteenth century. An NGO with a small secretariat based in Geneva, Switzerland, ISO has national standard-setting bodies, one for each country, as members. Most national bodies are also made up of members, which may include trade associations, professional societies, government agencies, firms, universities, and even individuals. The number of members can differ by an order of magnitude, a reflection of different national histories as well as the differing sizes of national populations:

> For example, the membership of the American National Standards Institute (ANSI) includes approximately 1,300 corporations, about 260 technical, professional, and industrial groups, 30 government agencies, dozens of universities, several towns, and even a few foreign companies. Canada's national standards body ... lists 8,000 members; Japan's (JISC [Japan Industrial Standards Committee]) 11,000 members; and the United Kingdom's BSI [British Standards Institute] a staggering 23,000 members. For each of these, many members are associations that themselves have thousands or tens of thousands of members.[27]

The oldest national bodies typically trace their origin to an early twentieth-century agreement among national engineering societies (of civil engineers, mechanical engineers, electrical engineers, and others). Many of these societies were, themselves, early innovators in voluntary consensus standard setting. BSI, the first national society, was founded this way in 1901 and ANSI in 1918.

At the time of BSI's founding, no such general body yet existed to foster international standards, but standardizing activity around network technologies such as railroads, telegraph, and electricity had occurred across countries, especially in Europe, complementing intergovernmental work on weights and measures, money, banking transactions, and various areas of public administration. In fact, the original network of late nineteenth-century intergovernmental organizations and their successors, the "specialized agencies" of the League of Nations and then the United Nations, were—and sometimes still are—referred to as "standard setting agencies."[28]

Many of the intergovernmental conferences that created these earlier intergovernmental organizations took place at the frequent "international exhibitions," the world's fairs.[29] Often, international groups of scientists and engineers would meet at the fairs to try to set fundamental standards in those fields that governments would not tackle.

The 1904 world's fair in St. Louis became a turning point in the history of international institutions for standardization. After more than 20 years of international meetings aimed at establishing and naming standard electrical units—the ohm, the watt, etc.—the delegates to the 1904 International Electrical Congress passed a resolution calling for the establishment of an ongoing international body to continue and expand on their work.[30] Two years later, a special meeting in London created the non-governmental International Electrotechnical Commission (IEC) and placed a young British electrical engineer, Charles Le Maistre, in charge of its London office.[31] In 1906, Le Maistre also held administrative positions in the British professional association of electrical engineers and in the British Engineering Standards Committee, the organization that would become BSI. He would remain at the center of the movement for international standardization until his death in 1953, when he still held the position of general secretary of the IEC.[32]

The bodies linked by Le Maistre—the IEC and the British national committee—developed many of the techniques and institutional mechanisms that came to typify international standard setting and that are today embodied in ISO. The early IEC included representatives of industry, of the engineering professions, and of governments. Alexander Siemens, head of the British division of the German company Siemens and the nephew of its founder and telegraphic pioneer Werner von Siemens, chaired its founding meeting, and Ichisuke Fujioka, "the Father of Electricity of Japan" and the founder of Toshiba, represented Japan.[33] Such industry representatives undoubtedly reinforced the group's agreement "that manufacturing interests should be represented on the Local Committees," the national bodies that would be the official members of the IEC.[34] The same meeting adopted the British engineers' precedent of doing most of its work through committees that could act with unusual authority and would be small enough to function largely by correspondence.[35] In 1911, IEC established its first technical committee, IEC/TC-1, to deal with "matters of terminology and definition in the electrotechnical domain."[36] Decisions of IEC technical committees had to be ratified by the national bodies that made up the commission, each country with a single vote. Decisions would be published as IEC standards only when no one objected; split decisions would be published with the names of countries voting for and against them.

For the next 40 years, the IEC's Charles Le Maistre pressed for the application of these principles to all efforts to establish industrial standards. He and other early standard-setters envisioned the creation of something like today's ISO network long before the First World War, but agreement would not be reached until after the Second World War. The standard setters' initial focus was more on the establishment of non-governmental national standards bodies throughout the industrialized world. While both the Depression and the Second World War caused businesses and governments to turn inward, concentrating on the domestic market, the international standards movement still found opportunities to extend cooperation among the national standards bodies and prepared the ground for the 1946 conference that established ISO.

ISO often describes Le Maistre as the central figure in the early evolution of today's global standards network, "the father of international standardization,"[37] but he did not act alone. He was part of what historian Winton Higgins calls a generation of "evangelical engineers."[38] Higgins writes that, immediately after the First World War

> in a spirit of internationalism, engineering associations in the foremost countries of the second industrial revolution—particularly the USA, Germany, Sweden, and Britain—generated enormous enthusiasm around the project of optimising the application of mass-production principles, not least standardisation, to civilian industries. They ... mobilised in several evangelising "movements," at first the "standardisation movement" and the broader "rationalisation movement," and in the second half of the twenties, the "simplified practice movement."[39]

"Simplified practice" had its greatest champion in Herbert Hoover, the engineer who was elected US president in 1928, after revolutionizing business–government relations as Secretary of Commerce. Hoover was also one of the leading US advocates of standardization. In fact, when he died in 1964, Thomas Balogh, the economist who was chief science advisor to Britain's Labour government, called Hoover "the greatest American of the century" because of the impact of his promotion of industrial standards.[40] Yet, as president, Hoover failed to stem the tide of the Depression. That failure, and the similar failure of the more grandiose engineering movements in other parts of the world, may help explain why two of the three movements mentioned above are no longer as familiar.[41] Only the standardizing movement continued long after the others faded away.

Its survival may have something to do with the ways in which its collective identity differed from those of the related movements. The standardizers were, they believed, *practical, internationalist, modest, democratic,* and *process-oriented* people who *served the common good.*

In contrast to many of the "evangelical engineers," the standardizers of the early twentieth century saw themselves as *practical* men. They learned from, but, nonetheless, defined themselves as distinct from, the nineteenth-century scientists who had pioneered the practice of holding periodic conferences to establish fundamental units of measurement. The standardizers wanted science to be applied to improving human life. They were engineers, not scientists. Moreover, as time went on, they were not just *any* engineers; they were those engineers who wanted standards to be set and adopted. They differed from those engineers who wanted to exclude the business users of standards from the deliberation of experts who would only be satisfied with those standards that were optimal or the most elegant. Le Maistre, for example, played a particularly critical role in convincing US engineers to accept businessmen into the deliberations of the organization that would become ANSI.[42] This practical orientation assured that the standards movement would quickly grow beyond professional engineers to include all those who had become convinced of the value of standard setting.

Higgins is certainly correct to say that the early standardizers were internationalists from the start. He gives a humorous example of this in the menu for a lavish picnic organized for Le Maistre by the Australian standards body when he was on a proselytizing visit from London in 1932. The main course was "'Sandwiches (to Standard Specifications)'" alongside "'*Salade de la Société Nations,*'" but there was also "'Simplified Practice—Billy Tea' and '*Gâteau à Boomerang,*'" indications that there was no contradiction between internationalism and a commitment to one's own nation.[43] After all, until the formation of ISO, the focal organizations for standardizers were *national* standard setting bodies; ISO's international predecessors did relatively little of the work of standardization. The standardizers were not the kind of utopian internationalists who would be marginalized by the failure of the League of Nations and the early twentieth-century peace movements.[44]

Some of those marginalized liberal internationalists had visions as grand as that of Hoover's movement for administrative simplification. In contrast, throughout the Depression, the claims of the standardizers became more modest, centering on arguments about the significance of standard setting to shaping desirable innovation and, thus, contributing to industrial development and general prosperity. Later standardizers would call themselves "austere and fussy"[45] and even "geeks."[46]

Nonetheless, as political scientist Samuel Krislov points out, "the nominal diffidence of engineering standardizers" might conceal "the strong Uriah Heep aspect of the approach ... Standardization is just the ultimate form that a ... deification of the 'engineer' can take ... In contradistinction, the profit motive has room for consumerist preferences, and for production for use, not design."[47]

Yet, this is not what happened with the movement as a whole. By the 1930s, the standardization bodies in all of Higgins's "foremost countries of the second industrial revolution" (and in many others) had long given up on the notion that the best standards were set by engineers alone. Instead, they followed what Le Maistre called the "*democratic* and progressive principles" to bring together "the producer and the consumer, including the technical officers of the large spending departments of the government and the great classification societies."[48]

While, as far as we know, no one inside the standards movement has ever developed a rigorous theory of the particular kind of deliberative democracy that is their ideal,[49] the evidence of the centrality of that shared ideal is extensive. It appears in the title of ISO's official history, *Friendship Among Equals*, and is in almost every chapter, from immediate post-Second World War worries about whether it would be possible "to create a new organization which would do the work of standardization in a democratic way, and not cost too much,"[50] to jokes about the national delegate who was voted down and cried, "'And you call that democracy!,'" because he had expected the chair to follow the more deliberative, consensus rule.[51]

These *process-oriented* men and women share justifications for every aspect of system that they champion: The division of work across technical committees reflects the functional division of the world in which standards may be needed and it points to the specific expertise relevant to any field. The inclusion of representatives of all stakeholders and the ideal of decision by consensus help assure that standards are legitimate and, hence, widely adopted. The voluntary nature of the standards produced assures that they would not impede innovation; inventors and entrepreneurs are spared the rigidity of autocratic regulation. This process orientation distinguishes those in the standards movement from all those who are happy to accept standards arrived at by other means—by the imposition of government or through the exercise of the market power of leading firms.

Finally, the standardization movement has always seen itself as serving a higher public good. The voluntary consensus process is considered so desirable because it creates "better" (in some utilitarian sense) standards than those achieved by any other methods. Charles Le Maistre often used explicitly utilitarian language to explain his mission: "In its broadest aspect it [standardization] may be said to imply, the introduction, through collective effort of economical measures of manufacture, not so much with the idea of gaining individual dividends as of unifying the needs of industry and thus bringing about the greatest good for the greatest number."[52]

To reach "the greatest number" required that standardization bodies be set up all over the world so that, throughout the interwar years, Le Maistre traveled extensively, urging the establishment of national bodies throughout the British Commonwealth and in France,[53] while US engineers lobbied for their creation throughout Latin America.[54] In 1926, most of the existing national bodies created ISO's predecessor, the International Federation of National Standardization Associations, known as the "ISA." The ISA, like the IEC and the national bodies, organized its work through technical committees, but the ISA committee's job was only to exchange information, not to agree on new standards. That would be done only "after the new organization had considerable experience."[55]

ISA never gained that experience. The federation never overcame the division between the "inch" and the "metric" countries, with Canada, Great Britain, and the United States on one side and the rest of ISA (Austria, Belgium, Czechoslovakia, France, Germany, Holland, Italy, Japan, Sweden, and Switzerland) on the other. In fact, one of ISA's few triumphs was agreement on a standard inch/millimeter conversion ratio.[56] Moreover, in the early years, Britain and Canada had little active support from the United States. In the 1920s, the US association was suffering financial problems and only agreed to join ISA in October 1929, less than two weeks before the stock market crash that ushered in the Great Depression.

Nevertheless, some consequences of ISA's work remain. The federation recommended a global standard for putting sound on motion picture film, something that immediately proved to be of great importance to one of the few internationally oriented US industries of the 1930s.[57] Other ISA legacies include the sizing of paper (A2, A4, etc.) worked out by the German national standards body which provided the secretariat of the ISA technical committee[58] and the 1940 recommendation that the prefix "nano-" to refer to 10^{-9}, one of the last decisions of an ISA technical committee. A half-century later, ISA's prefix would be used to name one of today's most active industrial frontiers, nanotechnology.[59]

ISA ceased functioning during the Second World War, but, in 1943, BSI began pushing for a new body "to 'spark plug' cooperation between the allied belligerent countries in standardization matters as an aid to production and use ... [and] secure the maximum possible coordination of standards necessary for the war efforts and the immediate post-war period."[60] The Allies, including the Latin American non-combatant "United Nations" (as the anti-fascist alliance called itself) created the UN Standards Coordinating Committee (UNSCC) in July 1944, with Le Maistre as the director of its London office.[61]

UNSCC technical committees had accomplished very little by the time the war ended. They continued to function, but discussion immediately turned to creating a more permanent successor organization. As its name indicates, UNSCC only had a mandate to coordinate national standards, not to create international ones. The war had highlighted the need for greater international standardization. According to the *Economist*, differences between British and American standards for screw threads alone added at least £25 million to the cost of the war.[62] The *Economist* argued that neither UNSCC (which included no former enemy, occupied, or neutral countries) nor the moribund ISA (dominated by the metric bloc) would encourage the economic recovery of all; a new organization was needed. The same position was widely shared by engineers and industrialists on both sides of the Atlantic.

ISO was formed in a series of meetings taking place in New York, Paris, and London from October 1945 (right after the end of hostilities) to October 1946. The meetings excluded only the defeated powers and established an organization that resembled both the IEC and ISA. ISO's technical committees were, from the beginning, empowered to publish recommended international standards—initially called "recommendations"—making it more powerful than the UN "Coordinating" Committee. ISO's constitution also allowed it to coordinate—not supersede—the IEC, treating it as an autonomous "technical division" of the larger organization. Le Maistre, who chaired the 1946 London meeting, helped finesse a number of conflicts—between the "inch" and metric blocs, with the Soviet Union (which insisted that Russian be treated as one of ISO's languages, along with English and French), and over the legal status of the ISA (abolished) and the location of ISO headquarters (Geneva narrowly defeated Montreal).[63]

ISO's three eras: gaining capacity, building a world market, and expanding scope

Le Maistre, like many of the early champions of industrial standards, passed away during the "golden years" of rapid global economic growth in the 1950s and early 1960s.[64] (Recall that Le Maistre died in 1953,

Hoover in 1964.) They lived to see ISO develop the capacity to be the global standard setter that they had imagined, but not to exercise that role fully. That major transition, which allowed ISO to help build a world market, took place between 1964 and 1986, a period that coincides with the predominance within the organization of a Swedish standard setter, Olle Sturén, who chaired the committee that systematically redirected ISO's work in the mid-1960s and then served as the organization's chief from 1969 through 1986. After Sturén's retirement, ISO continued to grow and to expand the scope of its activities into fields far removed from the nuts and bolts work of the earlier eras.

Gaining capacity, 1947–1964

In 1964, at the end of the first era, ISO was largely a European organization (Table 1.1). Although its membership consisted of national standard setting bodies throughout the world, fewer than half of these bodies participated in large numbers of ISO's technical committees. With the exception of Australia, Canada, India, Israel, and the United States, all of the major participants were European.

If we consider those who contributed the most staffing to the organization, this picture is even clearer. ISO relies upon its member organizations to provide the secretariats of the different committees. Taken together, just two bodies, BSI and the French standards association (AFNOR) provided almost half (92 of 227) of the secretariats of the technical committees and their subcommittees; other Western European countries, especially the Netherlands, took on tasks equally disproportionate to their populations. France and the UK also hosted a disproportionate number of the meetings of the committees as well. Moreover, given the membership of the technical committees, it is not surprising that, even when they met outside of Paris or London, they still most often met in Western Europe (Table 1.2).

In 1958, a relatively young Olle Sturén—who at 38 had just become head of the Swedish Standards Institute (SIS)—wrote that Western Europe had a much greater interest in having global standards than the USA or Eastern Europe did because Western European nations, unlike the COMECON (Council for Mutual Economic Assistance) nations or the continental USA, must sell to global markets.[65] In 1969, shortly after he became ISO secretary general, Sturén looked back on these years of European dominance as ISO's childhood. "If we look at ISO as a child born in 1947," he said, "the child's education is finished."[66]

The early ISO, Sturén argued, had done much of global significance under Western Europe's special tutelage. The organization had finally

Table 1.1 ISO members in 1964 (50)

Major member bodies (22)

Country	TC participation	Secretariats held
Australia	41	1
Austria	42	2
Belgium	75	13
Bulgaria	40	0
Canada	49	0
Czechoslovakia	82	2
France	106	44
Germany	101	21
Hungary	45	1
India	77	7
Israel	52	1
Italy	89	10
Netherlands	92	20
Poland	65	6
Portugal	43	3
Romania	45	2
Spain	43	0
Switzerland	57	12
Sweden	85	4
UK	106	48
USA	66	21
USSR	60	4

Other members (27 with an average TC participation of 8)

Albania	Indonesia	New Zealand
Argentina	Iran	Norway
Brazil	Ireland	Pakistan
Burma	Japan	Peru
Chile	Korea, D.P.R.	South Africa
Colombia	Korea, Republic	Turkey
Denmark	Lebanon	United Arab Republic
Finland	Mexico	Venezuela
Greece	Morocco	Yugoslavia

Source: "The ISO Technical Committees Shown in Figures 1947–1964." ISO/
GA-1964-8, 12–13.

established a globally accepted common terminology of measurements
and nomenclature as well as common ways of testing different basic
materials, including steel, cement, and plastics. "In the field of basic
mechanical engineering, ISO inherited the ISA program," and basically completed it; in 1969, "nuts and bolts" problems of mechanical
incompatibilities were becoming a thing of the past.[67]

Table 1.2 Location of ISO technical committee meetings, 1947–63 (10 most frequent locales)

City	Meetings
Paris	398
London	379
The Hague	111
Zurich	65
Brussels	60
Milan	59
Düsseldorf	44
New York	44
Turin	42
Berlin	38

Source: "The ISO Technical Committees Shown in Figures 1947–64," ISO/GA-1964–8, 22–23.

Building a world market, 1964–1986

Nevertheless, now there was a much larger agenda that Sturén knew well. He had first become heavily involved in ISO in 1964, when he was asked to chair a study group to respond to a challenge laid down by NEN, the Nederlands Normalisatie-instituut. The Dutch were convinced that the world economy was about to enter a new phase, what we would now call the phase of "globalization." Political nationalism and even economic nationalism might exist for many generations, but, as Sturén put it, "[O]ne must face the fact that industrial nationalism is about to disappear."[68] ISO charged his committee—called "NEDCO (the Netherlands Committee, so to speak)"[69]—with five broad responsibilities. They were to figure out how ISO could: (1) stop the duplication of effort by national standards bodies—there was no reason for the Dutch to create a standard for plastic milk bottles that differed from the one already created by the Danes or the Italians; (2) reduce the time needed to create standards in new technological fields; (3) cooperate more effectively with the European Economic Community and similar regional bodies, with increasingly vocal consumer groups, with UN agencies that were promoting industrialization throughout the world, and with the GATT (the General Agreement on Tariffs and Trade), which was rapidly creating a global market in industrial goods; (4) work more effectively with the still largely autonomous IEC, which had a leading role to play in the rapidly changing field of telecommunications; and (5) "spread knowledge and proper use of standardization in non-technical circles," that is, do a better job of public relations.[70] NEDCO's recommendations about these topics became ISO's agenda for the next two decades.

One of the simple, but important ways in which the organization changed its public relations after NEDCO was to rename its "recommendations" as "international standards" in 1972. A decade later, most of the duplication among national standards bodies had been eliminated. In fact, by the 1980s, most of the time and effort expended by many of the most active national bodies was directed toward the development of global standards and many "national" or "European" standards were simply word-for-word adoptions of ISO or IEC documents.[71]

Also, by the early 1980s, ISO had developed very close relations with the UN, which often provided technical assistance for the establishment of national standards bodies. Sturén himself had gotten his start in the international standards business in the early 1950s when he worked for the UN in Turkey providing the technical assistance needed to establish the national standards body there. He took a special interest in encouraging similar developments in other parts of the world, even if doing so meant a change in the nature of ISO. Because many developing countries established standards bodies as agencies of government, ISO began to look less like an NGO and more like a traditional intergovernmental organization. By the 1980s, due to the growth in membership from the developing world, the majority of ISO members were government agencies, not NGOs.[72]

In the 1970s and 1980s ISO also developed a close working relationship with the GATT. In 1979, in an effort to reduce non-tariff barriers to trade, GATT adopted a standards code that required its members to rely on international standards as the basis for their own technical regulations. This change did not necessarily mean that ISO standards automatically had the force of international law, but it did mean that GATT members had to develop very strong arguments if they did not adopt those standards as their own.[73]

Many accounts of ISO during this second period—this era of building a world market—emphasize the organization's role in standardizing the physical infrastructure of today's global economy, especially its impact on containerized shipping.[74] Chapter 3 discusses that role. It was during this second era that ISO began affecting almost every sector of the global economy. The steady growth in ISO standards that began in the late 1960s (see Figure 1.1) tells part of the story, but in 1997 Olle Sturén emphasized two other facts in looking back. The first was that by 1977, ISO had gained the "de facto monopoly" on setting international industrial standards in most sectors that it still has today. The major exceptions were pharmaceuticals, where the World Health

Organization (WHO) played the lead role; automobile safety, where the UN Economic Commission for Europe still maintained a position that it seized immediately after the Second World War; and telecommunications and information technology, where ISO shared its position with the IEC and the International Telecommunications Union (ITU).[75] Second, and more significantly in Sturén's mind, most new industrial standards since the 1980s had been international standards.

Expanding scope, 1987–2008

In the most recent era, the one that began in the late 1980s, ISO has entered new realms. It has come to play a major role in setting standards for quality management and extending their application into environmental fields and into more general areas of corporate social responsibility. Today, ISO's web site seems to define the organization as focusing on these topics.[76] At the beginning of 2008, when the page still wished visitors "A Very Happy and Prosperous New Year," its three "latest news" stories were about improving the quality of water services to consumers, fighting climate change, and improving quality management in the international oil and gas industries. Only ISO 9000 (the quality management standard), ISO 14000 (the environmental standard), and

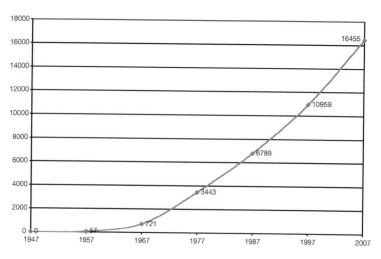

Source: ISO annual reports

Figure 1.1 Number of ISO standards.
Source: ISO annual reports

the still-to-be-finalized ISO 26000 on social responsibility (of ISO's more than 25,000 standards or standards-in-development) had direct links from the home page.

This new ISO has its roots in the second era. In Sturén's first address as secretary general, in 1969, he insisted, "ISO should take on work on water and air pollution, and noise levels, without delay"[77] and the standard that would become ISO 9000 was already fully formulated by BSI in the late 1970s.[78] (These fields of ISO's greatest recent expansion are the topics of Chapter 4.)

At the same time that ISO moved into, and had great success in, these new fields, its traditional role—that of setting the standards that shape innovation in cutting edge industries—may have been curtailed. Innovation in the new industries of the Information Age takes place so rapidly that the relatively slow system of setting standards by consensus in committees that include all stakeholders may be too slow. In 1997, one of the standards gurus in the information technology (IT) field, Sun Microsystems' Carl F. Cargill, wrote:

> I do not believe that ISO can recapture the IT market, barring a collapse of the speed of change, but it can change to retain its strength in other markets. Unlike the ITU, its processes are mutable. Its tragic flaw, however, is its belief in the fundamental goodness and purity of its process, and its unwillingness to change that process to match the change in the environment.[79]

Throughout the twentieth century, ISO and its predecessors were sustained by a social movement; those "evangelical engineers," many of them in cutting-edge industries, were committed to a larger social good than their own pecuniary interests or those of the company that employed them. Much of that same missionary zeal now appears in the computer field's Open Source movement—a movement that creates standards that are voluntary, but not reached through consensus. Chapter 5 looks at the battle among IT standards setters in the recent era, and at ISO's place within those battles. We argue that what may be emerging is less a transformation of ISO, than a transformation of the larger voluntary consensus process.

Conclusion

ISO emerged in response to issues that exist in all economies because standards both help determine boundaries of a trading area as well as the kinds of innovation that go on within it. By 1900, many engineers throughout the industrial world had become convinced that setting voluntary standards through committees of stakeholders was preferable to reliance on governments or the market alone. These standard setters worked to create the institutions—national, regional, and global—to allow such work to take place. ISO, formed immediately after the Second World War, was the ultimate result. Throughout its 60-year history, ISO first developed the capacity to set international standards, then focused on helping create a global market for industrial goods, and then shifted its attention to include the management standards for which it is most widely known today.

2   How ISO works

ISO's leaders have, at times, spoken about the organization as if it were almost part of the United Nations (UN) family,[1] but current practice is to call it "a non-governmental organization [NGO] that *forms a bridge between the public and private sectors* ... [M]any of its member[s] ... are part of the governmental structure of their countries ... [O]ther members have their roots uniquely in the private sector, having been set up by national partnerships of industry associations."[2] About two-thirds of ISO's 158 member organizations are part of their country's central government; the rest are NGOs.[3]

ISO conducts almost all of its work through technical committees that focus on specific topics. Each of its about 230 committees and 500 subcommittees has a rotating secretariat provided by one of the ISO member bodies. The committees conduct much of their discussion electronically[4] and when they meet face-to-face, they usually do so only for a day or two at a time. In 2008, about one-third of ISO's technical committees and subcommittees met in more than 90 cities spread across 34 countries and six continents.[5]

On top of the large committee structure rests a 150-person secretariat in Geneva, one much smaller than those of most of the UN Specialized Agencies based in the same city. Nonetheless, the vastness and complexity of ISO's decentralized structure means that the number of people actively working on establishing new international agreements throughout the ISO network is probably larger than the staff of the entire UN system.

The organization's highly decentralized structure somewhat obscures the relatively complex way in which the work of voluntary standard setting is funded. Ultimately, much of the funding comes from the major consumers of standards, the firms and other organizations that adopt them.

Similarly, ISO's insistence on the *voluntary* nature of its standards— for example, the ISO web site states that "*ISO itself does not regulate or legislate*"[6]—somewhat obscures a more complex reality. Most ISO standards become obligatory for at least some organizations because the standards are cited in national legislation and international conventions. This chapter concludes with a discussion of the range of ways in which ISO standards become part of global governance.

The ISO network and its voluntary consensus process: the actors and why they are involved

ISO has 158 national standard setting bodies, spread across the world, as members. Of these, about 35 unusually active members, which may be designated major member bodies, each take part in hundreds of different technical committees and their subcommittees. Together, this group provides almost all the secretariats. About twice as many member bodies, around 70 of the remaining 123, are more selectively active; they each take part in the limited number of technical committees that affect the economic sectors in which their country is the most involved. For example, the Ghana Standards Board represents a country whose major exports include cocoa and other products of the tropical rainforest. The board takes part in only 12 committees and subcommittees overall, and is especially active in the committees concerned with food products (TC-34), timber (TC-218), and environmental management (TC-207).[7]

In addition to these 105 regular members, ISO has 42 "correspondent members" from countries that are just developing independent national standards activities. These members rarely take active part in technical committees and are usually involved in only a few. Correspondent members do not have a right to take part in developing ISO's overall policies, but they are kept informed about all of the work that is of interest to them. Members in this group include countries that are not sovereign, but that have well established communities of engineers (e.g. Hong Kong and Palestine); some former Soviet republics with significant numbers of engineers but whose independent standards' bodies are relatively new; and many developing countries with almost no industrial base.

Finally, 11 "subscriber members" pay nominal membership fees. Most are countries with very small economies, such as landlocked Lesotho and many of the Caribbean island states. Box 2.1 details the ISO membership for 2008.

As we noted in Chapter 1, many of the regular members of ISO are organized in the same way that ISO is: they are organizations of organizations. Even some national bodies that are part of their central governments are organized this way. The Japan Industrial Standards

Box 2.1 ISO members in 2008 (158)

Major member bodies (35)

Country	Acronym	TC participation	Secretariats held
Argentina	IRAM	304	0
Australia	SA	534	24
Austria	ON	527	4
Belgium	NBN*	607	7
Brazil	ABNT	436	3
Bulgaria	BDS*	339	0
Canada	SCC*	379	20
China	SAC*	696	22
Czech Republic	CNI	573	1
Denmark	DS	380	6
Finland	SFS	526	2
France	AFNOR	730	82
Germany	DIN	728	107
Hungary	MSZT	507	0
India	BIS*	595	10
Ireland	NSAI*	386	0
Italy	UNI	660	20
Japan	JISC*	669	43
Korea, Republic of	KATS*	696	13
Mexico	DGN*	317	0
Netherlands	NEN	572	20
Norway	SN	401	15
Poland	PKN	637	7
Portugal	IPQ*	340	1
Romania	ASRO	568	0
Russian Federation	GOST R*	606	7
Serbia	ISS*	443	0
Slovakia	SUTN*	440	0
South Africa	SABS	387	4
Spain	AENOR	661	7
Sweden	SIS	535	19
Switzerland	SNV	515	16
Turkey	TSE	349	2
United Kingdom	BSI	720	85
USA	ANSI	617	117

Note:
* A body that, in 2007, was considered part of the central government by the World Trade Organization.

Box continued on next page

Other member bodies (70 with an average TC participation of 82)

Algeria	Libya
Armenia	Lithuania
Azerbaijan	Luxembourg
Bahrain	Macedonia
Bangladesh	Malaysia
Barbados	Malta
Belarus	Mauritius
Bosnia and Herzegovina	Mongolia
Botswana	Morocco
Chile	New Zealand
Colombia	Nigeria
Congo, D.R.	Oman
Costa Rica	Pakistan
Côte-d'Ivoire	Panama
Croatia	Peru
Cuba	Philippines
Cyprus	Qatar
Ecuador	Saint Lucia
Egypt	Saudi Arabia
Ethiopia	Singapore
Fiji	Slovenia
Ghana	Sri Lanka
Greece	Sudan
Iceland	Syria
Indonesia	Tanzania
Iran	Thailand
Iraq	Trinidad and Tobago
Israel	Tunisia
Jamaica	Ukraine
Jordan	United Arab Emirates
Kazakhstan	Uruguay
Kenya	Uzbekistan
Korea, D.P.R.	Venezuela
Kuwait	Vietnam
Lebanon	Zimbabwe

Subscriber members (11)

Antigua and Barbuda	Honduras
Burundi	Lao People's Democratic Republic
Cambodia	Lesotho
Dominica	Saint Vincent and the Grenadines
Eritrea	Suriname
Guyana	

Correspondent members (42 with an average TC participation of 7)

Afghanistan	Malawi
Albania	Moldova
Angola	Montenegro
Benin	Mozambique
Bhutan	Myanmar
Bolivia	Namibia
Brunei	Nepal
Burkina Faso	Nicaragua
Cameroon	Palestine
Dominican Republic	Papua New Guinea
El Salvador	Paraguay
Eritrea	Rwanda
Estonia	Senegal
Gabon	Seychelles
Georgia	Swaziland
Guatemala	Tajikistan
Hong Kong	Togo
Kyrgyzstan	Turkmenistan
Latvia	Uganda
Macau, China	Yemen
Madagascar	Zambia

Source: "ISO members," www.iso.org/iso_members.

Committee's 11,000 members include trade associations, professional societies, and government agencies, many of which also create standards or did so in the past. The standard setting bodies at all levels tend to work in the same way: they bring together representatives of their members toward consensus on documents (literally, these documents *are* "standards") that define specific qualities of products (such as the sizes of nuts and bolts), services, or business practices. The aim is to provide standards that will be widely and *voluntarily* adopted by organizations that produce the specific product or service or engage in the specific business practice.

Most standard setting bodies do their work through those "technical committees" that focus on a particular range of products, services, or practices. Many of the committees meet over many years, not only to set standards, but to amend them as conditions change. The oldest of ISO's technical committees (TC-1 Screw threads) continues the work of groups that had been meeting for decades before ISO's formation.[8] The most active of ISO's technical committees, JTC-1 Information technology, is a committee run jointly with the International Electrotechnical Commission (IEC); JTC-1 has published more than 2,100 standards, more than twice the number of any other committee.[9]

ISO's technical committees are made up of "national delegations" recruited by the member body. Each delegation is expected to include experts on the technology in question and to be broadly representative of a host of stakeholders: (1) industry and trade associations, (2) science and academia, (3) national governments and their regulatory agencies, and (4) relevant NGOs such as environmental groups.

ISO rules require each national delegation "to take account of the views of the range of parties interested in the standard under development [and] ... present a consolidated, national consensus position to the technical committee."[10] Within ISO technical committees, then, each national delegation must, in theory, come to a consensus and vote as a whole. In fact, because the committee as a whole also operates on the basis of consensus, at any point before the end of the discussion, there are likely to be disagreements *within* national delegations and strong agreements among some members *across* delegations from different countries even when the official positions of their countries are at odds. The longest-serving ISO secretary general, Olle Sturén, often found the inability of national delegates to agree among themselves to be particularly vexing, especially when the issue was something as important as the size of freight containers or protocols for the electronic transfer of data![11]

Specific "consensus" rules differ a bit from one standard setting body to the next, but the underlying principle is the same. Harland Cleveland, the public administration expert who advocates using ISO methods to tackle a host of international problems, summarizes the norm: "Consensus," usually means, "the acquiescence of those who care [about a particular decision] supported by the apathy of those who don't."[12] ISO has a "one-country, one-vote" system. Two-thirds of the member bodies participating in a technical committee must vote in favor to send a draft standard forward. Under current rules, two-thirds of the member bodies participating in the committee must approve a standard and no more than a quarter may actively oppose it.[13]

Adherence to the standards published by ISO and similar bodies is officially voluntary, and that is the most important meaning of the word in the phrase "voluntary consensus standards." However, there are also important ways in which the work of the technical committees is "voluntary," as well.

Recall that ISO's Central Secretariat neither organizes nor pays for all the management and record keeping that is necessary to maintain the hundreds of technical committees and subcommittees. Instead, different member organizations volunteer to act as the secretariats for specific committees or subcommittees. (The same practice is replicated down the nested hierarchy of standard-setting organizations; for example, different national trade associations or professional societies volunteer to be the secretariats of technical committees organized by a national standard setter.) In ISO, the most active member bodies rotate the burden of such work among themselves.

Sometimes a decision to take on the cost of maintaining a secretariat has to do largely with what a country (or its key industries) might gain or lose. Thus, it may not be surprising that the Swiss regularly provide the secretariat for TC-114 Horology, since Swiss clock- and watch-makers have a precarious dominance of the global industry.[14] On the other hand, often volunteering seems to be a consequence of a country's identity—less a question of "what we might gain" and more a question of "who we are." For example, in ISO's early years, even though most of the technical committees were serviced by the earliest of the national bodies and those of the most industrialized nations, Nehru's India—the "modern nation" that Nehru *defined* in terms of its commitment to science and industrial progress—took on three committees and four subcommittees, a commitment only slightly less than that of Italy, and slightly more than that of Sweden.[15] More recently, the 2004 decision of the Swedish and Brazilian standards bodies to act as co-conveners of the working group on ISO 26000, the standard on corporate social responsibility, seems to have reflected convictions in both countries that their firms had some special knowledge and commitment to social responsibility (consider unusually rapid embrace of the UN's Global Compact by Brazilian firms) as well as the long-standing commitment of Sweden to improved relations between the First and the Third Worlds, a major purpose of the standard.[16] This aspect of the "volunteerism" in non-governmental standard setting is similar, and may be related to the *noblesse oblige* that convinced different nineteenth-century monarchs to act as sponsors and benefactors of the first generation of global intergovernmental organizations, including the ITU (International Telecommunication [originally "Telegraph"] Union) and ILO (International Labor Organization), often without the active support of their governments.[17]

The final, and perhaps most important, voluntary element of the global voluntary consensus standard system is the involvement of those who serve on the technical committees. One estimate put the number of people engaged in 2000 as over 100,000, at a time when ISO's paid staff numbered only 163. By this estimate the volunteer group would have been about as large as the paid staff of all the organizations within the UN system, the UN proper and all the UN Specialized Agencies including that of the World Bank, ILO, and ITU.[18]

Why do all these people volunteer? Well, for many, it is a part of their job. They are working for companies that a proposed standard will affect and they are paid by the company to sit as a representative of one of the stakeholders. Mark Nottingham, a computer standards professional in California, has set up a humorous Amazon. com web page for prospective "volunteers" of this sort. "So You'd Like to Be a Standards Geek" lists all the books and other paraphernalia you need to take part in the electronic discussion and roam the world attending the endless round of meetings. The second item on the list is Machiavelli's *Prince*, "It's short, sweet (well, not really) and gets you in the proper frame of mind for doing battle, er, gathering consensus."[19]

Of course, the company stakeholder representatives are not the only members of the technical committees. Some of the women and men on the committees, especially those placed there as "neutral experts" by the constituent standard setting bodies, are likely to be believers in standard setting per se. They may also view their role as important in reinforcing their expertise and stature in relevant technical communities. Even company representatives are likely to be "standards geeks," otherwise they probably would have wormed their ways into more comfortable jobs; as Nottingham points out, "One of the perks and millstones of being a standards person is constant travel. It's fun for a while, but separation from your family and familiarity with the Boeing and Airbus corporations' products wear quite quickly."[20] A generation earlier, Olle Sturén registered a similar complaint:

> Anyone who thinks that attendance at technical committee meetings is a comfortable, touristic experience is mistaken. Standards making is a hard profession and makes tremendous demands on participants if the standard is to be good and welcome for worldwide application. When sitting on an ISO committee you are often in the company of the best brains in the relevant industry, and somebody who is not completely confident technically may hesitate before contributing the mildest comment.[21]

All of which is to say that many different motivations are at play in any technical committee. Moreover, as we discuss later in this chapter, this is a major reason that the voluntary consensus process seems to work: it actually produce standards that are then widely adopted.

Agenda-setting power within ISO and the role of the Central Secretariat

ISO is overseen by a council and an annual meeting of the member bodies. The meeting elects a president and two vice presidents and appoints 18 member bodies to the ISO Council, which acts as the organization's governing board and meets at least twice each year. The membership of the council rotates, but it always includes the major national standard setting bodies such as AFNOR (the Association Française de Normalisation), ANSI (the American National Standards Institute), and BSI (the British Standards Institute). Immediately after the Second World War, ISO's original members agreed to give long-term seats to the standards bodies of the same Big Five powers that had been made permanent, veto-wielding members of the UN Security Council. However, the engineers who created ISO, unlike the diplomats who created the UN, decided that it would be good to remember that nothing is permanent—especially the relative prowess of industrialized countries—so ISO has always had a mechanism for reviewing its list of quasi-permanent council members.

The council appoints a rotating treasurer (who helps the board monitor the financial decisions of the profession staff) and a permanent secretary general, who is actually responsible for the day-to-day operation of ISO. The council is advised by standing committees on finance and on strategy (i.e. long-term planning) and by less permanent committees on policy development. In 2008, these included the Committee on Conformity Assessment (CASCO) and committees concerned with consumer policy and the developing countries. CASCO studies ways to assess the degree to which products, processes, services, and management systems conform to published standards.

The council also is advised by a handful of "strategic and technical advisory groups" that deal with issues that involve coordination across industrial sectors or fields in which ISO's long-term role has not yet been determined. One recent example is the field of information security, the subject of a committee that links ISO, the IEC, and the ITU.[22]

The various advisory groups and ISO's technical committees ostensibly report to the council, but they do so via the Technical Management Board, TMB. This board holds most of the agenda-setting power in ISO. The TMB's 10 members always include the most influential of the standard setting bodies, those that provide the secretariats for the most significant technical committees and those associated with the largest economies. In 2008 the members were AFNOR, ANSI, and BSI along with the standard setting bodies of Brazil, Canada, China, Germany,

Japan, the Netherlands, Norway, Spain, and South Africa. The TMB is chaired by one of ISO's rotating vice presidents.

In 2005, Ziva Patir, who was chair of the TMB and director general of the Standards Institution of Israel, explained that the TMB's purpose was to assure ISO's continued "global relevance" by entering new fields and by establishing working relationships with other standard-setters who are also involved in the same areas. She pointed to seven fields in which ISO was beginning to focus aggressively: (1) security, (2) social responsibility, (3) management systems, (4) food safety, (5) tourism, (6) nanotechnology, and (7) second-hand goods.[23]

This is a grab bag of issues. Some are on the global agenda due to the concerns of consumers (food safety) and progressive NGOs (social responsibility). One item on the list is a fundamentally new industrial field (nanotechnology), while another is a maturing field where an absence of some interoperability standards is causing widely recognized problems (management systems)—the traditional sort of problem dealt with by voluntary consensus standard setters. The others are just sectors experiencing rapid growth (security, tourism, and second-hand goods). What links these fields is Patir's, and the TMB's, sense that these are areas in which ISO *may* have a role to play in standard setting, and, perhaps even more significantly, if ISO does not stake out a claim to being the primary standard setter in these fields, other organizations will.

Given the agenda-setting significance of the TMB, the vice president who chairs it can play an important role in shaping what ISO becomes. The same is true of the heads of the most active member bodies. For example, there is some evidence that, in the early 1960s, the head of BSI (with the occasional support of the head of AFNOR) was individually responsible for the removal of ISO's first secretary general, the selection of his relatively short-lived replacement, and then the selection of Olle Sturén, who shaped ISO for the next 17 years.[24] Because ISO's presidents (who serve for only two years) often come from the most influential member bodies, they, too, can play a powerful role, but the source of their power is not the ISO presidency itself, which can sometimes just be an honor given to an important standard setter for a lifetime of work, something in the same way that the presidency of many academic associations honors the achievements of a senior scholar.

The ISO secretary general is also potentially quite powerful due to the position's unique role in connecting the member bodies and standard setters around the world. Sturén began the current practice of the secretary general traveling widely; he typically visited more than 10

member bodies on three continents every year.[25] His successors benefited from the establishment, in the 1990s, of seven regional groupings
of ISO members (originally for Africa, the Americas, the Arab region,
Europe, the Pacific Rim, Southeast Asia, and a "Euro-Asiatic" region
covering the former Soviet sphere). The meetings of these groups, according to the man who replaced Sturén, Lawrence Eicher, provided him
with, "greatly increased opportunities for communication and dialo-
gue,"[26] a much wider range of face-to-face meetings than his predecessor
had enjoyed.

The secretary general's power comes more from these connections
than from the position at the head of the modest Central Secretariat in
Geneva. The secretariat coordinates the standard-setting work being
done by the separate technical committees, oversees the (now largely
electronic) voting on draft standards, and completes the final editing of
new standards. Staff members also publish and sell ISO standards and
conduct public relations campaigns.

Of course, the way in which those campaigns define ISO's mission
and place in the world could, indeed, have a great deal of influence
over the long-term direction of the organization. ISO's information
campaigns can create expectations among members and among larger
publics about what ISO is and what it can do. The ISO 9000 series of
quality management standards has long been the focus of a very successful campaign.[27] More recently, Ziva Patir made a great deal of a
program of "Promoting Standards Through Art" in this regard,[28] but
it is not clear that this program has even been as successful as a much
older campaign to encourage the celebration of "World Standards
Day" (14 October). That campaign at least convinced a dozen countries to issue celebratory postage stamps between 1970 and 1995.[29]
Even ISO's newest public relations materials—such as its 2007 attempt
to rebrand itself as "the Interesting Stories Organization"—have a
slightly geeky quality that may limit their ability to mobilize new
demand for ISO services.[30]

The greatest influence of members of the ISO secretariat may come
from the fact that it is apparently a relatively congenial organization in
which to work, people stay a long time, and they develop a strong,
specialized organizational memory that must be invaluable to member
organization's representatives who are apt to change much more rapidly.
The official ISO history ends with a chapter by Roseline Barchietto, a
40-year employee, who reports, "I also have (maybe it is not nice to say
so) a good memory, particularly for figures, which is very useful
with 8,000 projects being processed. One of our bosses … always said:
'I don't need to have a computer because I already have a live one!'"[31]

Box 2.2   Destined to be ISO president?

Oliver R. Smoot served as ISO president in 2003 and 2004. Prior to that, he had served two years as chairman of ANSI. For most of his career, Smoot, an attorney specializing in computer law, worked as an officer of the Information Technology Industry Council, a trade association and an ANSI member. He was active in computer standard setting and regulation, serving on ISO's most active technical committee (JTC-1 Information technology) and in many positions in the Computer Law Association.

Smoot's name is well known among his fellow alumni of the Massachusetts Institute of Technology (MIT) and to many people in Boston and Cambridge, but not because of his work in setting *computer* standards. Back in 1958, when he was a freshman, Smoot and other new pledges to the Lambda Chi Alpha fraternity were required as part of their initiation to measure the bridge connecting MIT to Boston using Smoot's body as their ruler. The bridge proved to be "364.4 Smoots and an ear" long (about 0.6 kilometers). Each year, the chalk marks they made as they laid Smoot end-to-end are repainted by the latest Lambda Chi pledges and when the bridge was rebuilt in the late 1980s, specially-made Smoot-length slabs of pavement were laid to form the bridge's new sidewalks. The Smoot had become a fundamental measurement standard!

More recently, MIT alumni and students training for the Boston Marathon have been known to set their workouts in Smoots, and users of Google Earth can choose it as the unit in which they measure the world.

Sources: Robert Tavernor, *Smoot's Ear: The Measure of Humanity* (New Haven, Conn.: Yale University Press, 2007), xi–xvi; "MIT Spotlight: A Salute to Smoot," web.mit.edu/spotlight/smoot-salute/.

The development of specific standards

In theory, ISO's standard setting is demand driven. The organization is expected to set up new technical committees, approve new subcommittees, and suggest new areas of work when there is significant demand, say, from the companies that produce incompatible products, or, more likely, from the companies that purchase them! In fact, as the current grab bag of TMB interests suggests, ISO also plays an entrepreneurial role; it helps create the demand for the services it can provide. The secretary general, vice presidents, and the leaders of major national bodies are constantly looking for areas in which new standards might prove useful, especially fields in which ISO's deliberative process would have an advantage over other ways in which standards might be set.

Moreover, some very important ISO standards actually have been "supply driven." Consider ISO's entry into the quality management field through ISO 9000. Standards guru Carl Cargill calls ISO 9000 "a retread of an old US military standard on quality management and quality assurance from the 1960s that was rewritten by the British and then sold to ISO as the first of a series of 'management standards.'"[32] As we will see in Chapter 4, there is an almost religious dispute about the earliest origins of ISO 9000, but no one contests that the standard ISO adopted was essentially the one that BSI had designed and heavily promoted.

Whatever the impetus for a particular ISO standard, its production goes through a series of stages in which proposals are drafted and debated within a technical committee. The secretariat of the committee, the national body that has taken on that role, is responsible for organizing meetings, assigning particular drafting tasks, and conducting voting, much of which can now be done through the electronic system maintained by the Central Secretariat.

During technical committee discussions, the secretariat is required to be neutral and "disassociate itself from the national point of view,"[33] while each national delegation is expected to come to a consensus position even though it must include people reflecting fundamentally different interests. Under current ISO rules, the ability of national delegations to achieve an internal consensus may be aided by the fact that many trade associations and other interest groups are can now be directly represented within technical committees by more than 600 national and international NGOs, government bureaus, and intergovernmental organizations that need not be part of national delegations. Thus, for example, the Office Québécois de la Langue Française contributes to TC-37 Terminology and other language and content resources, the European Cork Federation takes part in the work of TC-87 Cork, and the American Oil Chemists' Society (a food oils group) works with three of the subcommittees of TC-34 Food products.[34]

After the members of a technical committee have agreed on a draft standard, it is made available to all member bodies, who have five months to comment and to vote on it. If no member objects, the technical committee merely has to respond to any comments and the standard is then published and distributed by the ISO Central Secretariat. If some members object, there is an additional period of two months for comment and voting. Assuming two-thirds of the members on the committee still support the standard, and no more than one-quarter oppose, it is published.

In the late 1980s, the production of a new standard within a technical committee typically took 72 months or six years. By 2002, that time had been reduced to 51 months (closer to four years), even though the average amount of documentation for each new ISO standard (the number of published pages it required) had almost tripled. This improvement may be attributable to the IT (information technology) explosion in the 1990s, when ISO committees began to be able to carry out much of their discussion and exchange of documents electronically.[35]

Past participants in ISO technical committees and scholars who have studied voluntary consensus standard setting have offered a series of plausible and compatible explanations of why such committees are so often able to reach consensus despite the many interests involved. One of the main arguments is that the committees provide a straightforward way to solve two kinds of problems that are faced by all standard setters.

The first, and simpler, kind arises when almost all producers or potential producers of a product or service (or users of a process) are convinced that there is a need for a standard: think of the nineteenth-century producers of nuts and bolts and all the manufacturers of mechanical equipment who had to rely on those parts. In this kind of case, the *particular* standard used for interconnection is not all that important; what is important is that there be *some* standard. These sorts of "coordination problems" can be solved relatively easily if those with technical expertise can agree on what they think is the "best"—or, at least, an "acceptable"—technology.[36] In fact, in the early days of the standards movement, many standard setters believed that the only problems that required their attention were such problems of coordination that could be solved by "expertise." This was one reason why many engineers felt it would just make things more complicated, it would muddy the waters, if the mere "users" of standards were brought into the voluntary consensus processes. Many engineers believed that they could do it by themselves, without representatives of the companies that were expect to adopt the standard.[37]

The men who created the non-governmental bodies that became part of ISO realized that they needed to include representatives of interested companies (e.g. delegates of their trade associations) if for no other reason than to help pay for the national bodies' central secretariats![38] Nonetheless, many of these new stakeholders were interested in more than just coordination problems. They were concerned with the kind of problems that might lead one to consider Machiavelli's *Prince* as one of the most important books for every standards geek to know. Game theorists call these problems of "cooperation" rather than of mere coordination. In the short term, many producer companies are perfectly happy with the solution, the "equilibrium," of incompatible standards. Back when videotape players were new, the companies who owned the patents on VHS wanted the chance to make money on their technology and so did Sony, who owned Betamax. Whenever there are incompatible standards, every company involved knows that there will be a quantifiable cost associated with moving to a single standard, at least for those companies that have to move, that "lose" a "standards war." Each company will want to minimize that cost, or find other ways to gain a competitive edge over its rivals.

Yet Randall Calvert, a political scientist who investigates cooperation problems, argues that, in the real world, most such problems are unusually complex, but that actually can make them easier to solve. In the complexity of the real world's "repeated games" the "players [e.g. potential users of a standard] face the problem of mutually identifying which of numerous possible 'good' equilibria to pursue." This creates what Calvert calls, "a *derived coordination problem.*"[39]

Consider companies like Sony back in the days of the Beta/VHS war or Apple in the early days of the personal computer; both of them may be thought of as having "lost" a major "standards war," but, in the long run, that "war" turned out just to be a temporary battle in a much longer conflict. A new business environment (created by VHS's dominance of videotape and Microsoft's ability to place its operating system on most personal computers) meant that the companies had to search for new products elsewhere and it is difficult to say whether the Apple or Sony of 2010 would be "better off" had they won their standards battle of 1970. Given that fact, it may even have been better had they not "fought the battle" (in the courts and in the marketplace) in the first place. It may have been advantageous if they had accepted a standard created by an ISO committee.

Of course, Sony and Apple did not know that at the time. Calvert wants us to think about the kinds of people who can convince parties that are facing such complex cooperation problems to choose to compete on one set of battlegrounds and not on others. In the case of standard setting, this "derived" or "second order" coordination problem is one of finding people who can convince all key stakeholders that they really do have an interest in, or a desire for, some shared standard.

In both the more complex situation, and the less complex one, Calvert points to leadership as providing the solution to the problem.

In the less complex case, participants in a consensus standards meeting can defer to any person or a small group who identifies something as "the standard" to which they should adhere. In the more complex case, the meetings' leaders may not only have to identify a common focal point, they may also have to act as mediators—private channels of messages from one party to another as well as sources of suggested compromises.[40] They might also, Calvert argues, have to act as "moral, inspirational, or 'transformational'" leaders, ones who promote different norms and different goals than the ones that the parties bring to the table. Contemporaries of many of the early leaders of the standard-setting movement, men like Charles Le Maistre (see pages 12–18), often described them in these terms.

Such leaders still exist. The IT "standards guru" Carl F. Cargill is someone often described in these terms. He is the one person whose book Mark Nottingham's "So You'd Like to Be a Standards Geek" lists as even more essential than Machiavelli's.[41] That makes sense, because the secret of the success of technical committees is that the inspired vision of a guru can trump the short-term realpolitik of a Machiavelli: a persuasive reframing of the problem can turn an intractable conflict among self-seeking company representatives into a deliberatively reached agreement on a technically viable solution that may shift competition in a socially valuable way.

What are the sources of the power of the leaders who take part in standard setting committees?[42] In the first case, when there is strong agreement on the need for a standard, it is most likely the perceived expertise of those committee members who are there due to their technical skills: "If a standard is desirable, let's go with the one suggested by the experts," (especially if the experts have taken into account all of the objections and suggestions offered by those of us who will be affected by the standard).

In the second case, where a more transformative, goal changing, kind of leadership may be needed, the ability to provide such transformative goals often derives from the active engagement of some of the standardizers in the larger "standards movement." Cargill, for example, is a "guru" not because he serves the interests of his employer, Sun Microsystems, particularly well, but because his vision extends beyond those interests; he has developed a new, historically embedded theory of contemporary voluntary consensus standard setting,[43] and he has even developed an agonized internal critique of the movement of which he is a part.[44]

To understand the deference that companies have given to engineers and other kinds of experts, and why those experts would voluntarily take part in such work, it may be useful to think of standardization as taking place within the kind of social field described by sociologist Pierre Bourdieu. Within that field are business leaders in the newest industries, men made powerful by their control of *economic capital* and bent on its further accumulation. Next to this group, and only slightly overlapping it, are more inter-related groups of scientists and engineers, holders of particular forms of *cultural capital*, of credentials and expertise, that they guard and try to augment. Taking part in important standardizing committees is not only a way to build cultural capital (a new credential that adds to an engineer's prestige vis-à-vis other engineers and even scientists), his expertise provides the kind of solution to which business people can easily defer.

The historian of the Australian standards movement, Winton Higgins, makes a similar claim about the motivations of the participants in technical committees, and relates it to a larger claim. According to Higgins, the transformative vision that sometimes solves problems faced by technical committees is not something that is limited to a few "gurus." Instead, the "democratic" process itself gives everyone the opportunity to see beyond their narrow interests or the even the disciplinary blinders of their expertise:

> By sitting on standards committees, many people enhance their professional competence and business contacts. They also take the opportunity to push the particular interest they represent on the committee in question. But beyond that, they immerse themselves in civic culture—the discipline of open discussion and argument between equals, compromise, and accepting the experience of being outvoted by one's peers. For those who come from hierarchical institutions, this experience is both novel and essential training for citizenship in a free society … Jürgen Habermas has revealed one of the secret strengths of the kind of deliberative decision-making that these standards bodies deploy. "Communicative rationality"—the outcome of open discussion and debate between equal individuals with different backgrounds—represents a superior rationality compared to the conclusions reached by experts and senior administrators in isolation, ones untested in debate. The standards produced by the typical standards body crystallise the communicative rationality that Habermas has in mind.[45]

Higgins might be overstating the case. On the other hand, many standard setters do speak and write about holding a kind of "public trust" when they take part in the work of ISO and its member bodies. Moreover, ISO's rules—especially the rule that national bodies are, themselves, expected to reach consensus before taking active part in global discussions, even though conflicting interests are represented at the national level—encourage standard setters think of themselves as trustees for a more general interest. In the 1946 Nobel Peace Prize Lecture, the eminent activist economist Emily Greene Balch called the "conception of a public trustee" a fruitful new idea that was beginning to play a role in "world cooperation in different fields." Balch pointed to its parallel in domestic affairs:

> In the United States, hospitals, colleges, all sorts of undertakings for the public welfare are carried on by boards of trustees entrusted with their administration, and they have an honorable record of devotion to their trust. The same man, who, trading in Wall Street, prides himself on his skill in making money, conceives of himself when he finds himself trusted to carry on a public service, as a public servant, and devotes his ability no longer to making money for himself but to the welfare of the park, or the research foundation, or other matter with which he now identifies himself.[46]

It is certainly true that, moving beyond any individual committee, the larger work of standard setting brings engineers and business people into larger social networks that enhance the third of Bourdieu's forms of capital, *social capital*, "the sum of the resources, actual or virtual, that accrue to an individual by virtue of possessing a durable network of more or less institutionalised relationships of mutual acquaintance and recognition."[47]

As we saw in Chapter 1, that larger social network was, from the beginning, a transnational movement. The norms and rhetoric of that movement, in turn, have continued to be useful resources deployed by leaders within those technical committees in which the issues are particularly contentious or complex. The existence of the standards movement is one important reason why ISO committees "work," why they actually produce consensus standards.

Paying for ISO standards and enforcing them

The products of ISO technical committees are the thousands of documents that ISO sells both as electronic files and as hardcopy. Each document provides the information necessary to make it possible for the purchaser to implement the standard in question. In most cases, the document is a final "International Standard," but ISO also sells draft international standards and other less consensus-based documents, which are, nonetheless, immediately implemented by many organizations.

ISO's sale of its standards covers about 40 percent of the budget of its Central Secretariat, which expended about US$34 million in 2006. The other 60 percent of the budget came from the dues of member bodies. ISO estimates that the 37 member bodies that provided secretariats for ISO technical committees that year contributed the equivalent of about US $136 million by carrying out that work.[48]

The member bodies, in turn, gain their revenue from a wide variety of sources. In 2006, Standards Australia (SA) received about two-thirds of its revenue from income on investments, 15 percent from royalties on its standards, and another 12 percent from its regular government grant.[49] SA is like a private university that has built a huge endowment and that expends only a small part of the income of that endowment each year. BSI, the oldest of the national standard setting bodies, today acts like more of a multinational corporation whose primary business is to assess and certify management systems and products of different companies around the world. Like Standards Australia, it makes a substantial "profit" (about US$25 million before taxes in 2006).[50] Most standards bodies, however, still rely on member dues, government grants, the sale of standards, and fees for "conformity assessment"—the business of assessing and certifying that standards are met. As a result, it is the purchasers of those standards and services, the standards' users, who ultimately pay for much of the secretariat work done by the ISO network.

Producers as well as users (and many others) pay for the time and expenses of the many participants in technical committees who are often subsidized by their companies or by the national body that appoints them. In 1977, Ole Sturén cited a US study that estimated the annual overall cost to the US for its involvement in ISO and IEC standards work as about US$500 million, in 2008 dollars.[51] Assuming that the number of men and women involved in such standard setting, globally, is the same today[52] and that the proportion of US involvement has remained constant, then the time and expenses of all those involved in international standard setting would be about US$7 billion per year, or about one-third of the total annual expenditures of the entire UN system.[53] This estimate seems very high. If we assume annual expenses of US$10,000 for each of the 100,000 people involved with ISO technical committees, the sum would be US$1 billion. The reality is probably somewhere between these two estimates.

Organizations adopt standards for a variety of reasons. Most often they do so simply because the standards help the organization achieve its goals—for example, a company can sell more of its products. Certainly, if the problem that led to the establishment of a standard in the first place was a coordination problem—a problem of agreeing that a standard should be set, but disagreeing on which standard it should be—then it is not surprising that the standard will be accepted voluntarily. Moreover, even in the case of those more complex cooperation problems, if a stakeholder has been involved in setting a standard, it will have a commitment to adopt it, and there is a great deal of social power to commitment.

In addition, there are often laws within and among nations that require organizations to adopt standards reached through voluntary consensus methods. In 1981, ANSI estimated that 80 percent of its standards had become mandatory in some jurisdictions due to their inclusion in national, state, or local legislation.[54] The pressures that ANSI identified as encouraging such an outcome in the US, a generation ago, have only grown and become more widespread and more focused on *international* standards. While Sturén was still ISO secretary general, the European Community and most of its members adopted the practice of having their regulatory bodies refer to international voluntary standards, specifications, and test methods rather than produce their own.[55] In the 1990s, the same practice was enacted into law in the US as part of the "Reinventing Government" initiative spearheaded by then vice president Al Gore and the OECD (Organization for Economic Cooperation and Development, the club of rich industrialized nations) has since recommended the practice to all its members.[56]

Even more significant is the way in which adherence to voluntary consensus standards has been written into international trade law. There are some ironies to the history of this development.

Back in the 1960s, the Europeans began to recognize that incompatible industrial standards might serve as non-tariff barriers to trade in the free trading area that trade officials were attempting to create within the European Economic Community and the linked European Free Trade Area. The US, in reaction, feared that the new Europe-wide standards regime could be a barrier to US entry into the European market, and demanded agreement on the GATT (General Agreement on Tariffs and Trade) Standards Code of 1979.[57]

Then, in the 1980s, when the European Community attempted to "complete" the internal market—in part by engaging in a much more aggressive process of reconciling incompatible industrial standards— the US again feared unfair exclusion from the European market, which fueled its interest in promoting the extensive and legally binding commitments that came with GATT's transformation into the World Trade Organization (WTO) in 1995. Now, WTO members are obligated to ensure that their regulations (at all levels, down to the very local) and any voluntary standards to which they refer do not create unnecessary obstacles to trade, which gives governments a great incentive to adopt ISO global standards as their own. Moreover, WTO members must ensure that their national, regional, and local standardizing bodies comply with a "Code of Good Practice" that prevents the creation of standards that might be a barrier to trade. This encourages national and regional standard setting bodies to do most of their work at a global level, because, for example, a new AFNOR standard that was developed, in fact, as an ISO standard is, prima facie, not designed to be an impediment to world trade, even if French legislation eventually gives it the authority of law within France.[58]

There is a final way in which ISO's "voluntary" standards become enforced. Some consider it the most important way: when companies and individuals that purchase products and services demand that they conform to international standards, even if a particular standard, per se, is irrelevant to the purchaser. As we discuss in Chapter 4, the great success of ISO 9000—"success" at least in terms of the number of organizations that have adopted it and the size of the industry that it has spawned—may largely have to do with the way in which its adoption serves as a signal to culturally and physically distant customers that "this company is serious" and, hence, a reliable business partner.

All of these mechanisms have contributed to the growing role of voluntary consensus standards in global governance, a role that may only increase in the years to come.

Conclusion

ISO is an unusual organization, the center of a huge network of volunteers, and its standards are, officially, merely recommendations that can be accepted or rejected. Yet, for some very good reasons, many organizations see ISO standards as obligatory, and their origins as obscure. ISO standards become obligatory through links to legislation and treaty law. The origins of ISO standards may seem obscure because they are complex. ISO, and all the organizations within its network, operate through technical committees made up of experts with complex personal motivations. Committee rules encourage members to seek standards that reflect broad interests. Nonetheless, power certainly plays a role in ISO work. A small group of ISO member bodies, mostly in Europe but also Japan and the United States, plays a disproportionate role within the organization and individuals have played decisive roles in shaping ISO's agenda, especially if they hold powerful roles within the organization.

3　Infrastructure for a global market

On 25 April 2006, BBC (British Broadcasting Corporation) business correspondent Toby Poston launched into a surprisingly long feature with this apology:

> There is perhaps no obvious reason to get excited about the fiftieth anniversary of a large metal box. Such containers are now an everyday sight, hauled by trucks, trains, and ships all over the world. But without them, it is very unlikely that we would all be buying Japanese TVs, Costa Rican bananas, Chinese underwear, or New Zealand lamb. In fact, globalization would probably not exist and the World Trade Organization [WTO] would have a lot less to talk about.[1]

And, of course, without ISO, there wouldn't be all those standard boxes.

When people in the standards movement enumerate the ISO's accomplishments, often the first thing they mention is the shipping container—and the resulting transformation of the physical infrastructure of international trade that enabled the integration and massive growth of the global economy over the last 30 years.[2] ISO's role was not just that of securing agreement on standard sizes for those boxes; ISO was also involved in setting standards for the ships and trains that carried the containers, the docks where they were loaded and unloaded, the cranes that lifted them, the training of the women and men who operated those cranes—the list of *physical* infrastructure goes on and on.

ISO also provided—and continues to provide—the standards needed to complete other aspects of the *technical* infrastructure of this new, global economy: standard documents for the transit of goods, standard bar-codes that could summarize and allow a quick electronic perusal of all that was in those documents, and even the standardized bank cards whose secure codes are the catalyst that starts the journey of so many of those boxes.

This chapter is about ISO's role in helping maintain the infrastructure of contemporary economic globalization. ISO officials see this as one of the central roles that ISO should continue to play even as the organization moves into new fields, such as quality management and environmental and social regulation.

We begin with ISO's current interpretation of that broader field and with ISO's official understanding of the activities within that field that are now its main purpose. Then we look in detail at the impact of the global shift to containerized shipping, and the role that ISO technical committees have played in that transformation of the physical infrastructure of the world economy. Finally, we consider the ways in which other ISO work has helped create other technical infrastructures that facilitate global trade, and the ways in which national members of ISO have helped provide essential technical infrastructure that ISO, itself, does not provide.

ISO's current niche within global governance

Since 2000, ISO documents have referred to the organization as a leader in building the "technical infrastructure" for "sustainable development" and for achieving the United Nations (UN) "Millennium Development Goals" (MDGs). Recall (page 5) that "technical infrastructure" refers, in large part, to a range of services associated with standard setting; technical infrastructure is the "software" that helps integrate a trading area, in this case, a *global* trading area. "Sustainable development" became the primary goal of many UN agencies in the 1980s and 1990s; the UN considers such development the outcome of a social and economic order that "fulfills human needs while maintaining the natural environment." The MDGs are eight targets for fulfilling human needs. These goals were agreed upon at a UN-led global summit of heads of government in 2000. They include cutting the number of people in extreme poverty in half and eliminating gender disparity in education at all levels by 2015.[3] By saying that ISO is a leader in the provision of technical infrastructure necessary to meet human needs in a sustainable way, the organization defines itself as having a specific role within "global governance" or "the management of common affairs at the global level."[4]

ISO does not claim to be the only organization critical to the provision of technical infrastructure at a global level. For example, ISO no longer claims a central position in the maintenance of fundamental standards—the business of agreeing on measures of the physical world—because, beginning in the 1960s, national governments have increasingly assigned the tasks associated with maintaining fundamental standards to two intergovernmental organizations based in Paris, the Bureau International des Poids et Mesures (BIPM) and the International Organization of Legal Metrology (OIML).[5] Nonetheless, while ISO's official statement of its limited role honors its fraternal neighbors, it is a bit disingenuous: An ISO technical committee—TC-12 Quantities, units, symbols, conversion factors—and its Danish and Swedish secretariats still maintain 17 subcommittees or "working groups" that convene all the 18 intergovernmental and non-governmental bodies that work on necessary updates to the global system of standard measures. The 18 include BIPM and OIML as well as, for example, the International Atomic Energy Agency, on the working group on atomic and nuclear physics. Moreover, TC-12 is constantly updating the international standards of quantities and units of space and time and fundamental properties (now called ISO 80000) that are administered or given legal status by the other international organizations.[6]

ISO has a similar self-understanding of its role relative to what some standardizers consider "the opposite end" of the technical infrastructure business: "conformity assessment." A joint ISO and International Electrotechnical Commission standard, ISO/IEC 17000, defines conformity assessment as a "demonstration that specified requirements relating to a process, system, person, or body are fulfilled,"[7] but ISO does not, itself, engage in such work.

Manufacturers sometimes have their own internal testing systems that certify that their work meets some standard, much in the way that universities in the United States of America certify that their students know particular fields because they have passed particular courses or exams, but, increasingly, in the private economy, conformity assessment is done through "third-party certification of inspection," similar to the process by which external examiners certify student knowledge in many other countries' university systems. In fact, many national standard setting bodies now make such third-party certification a major part of their own business.

Even more frequently, ISO members "certify the certifiers." The national bodies provide "accreditation," certification that third-party inspectors are qualified to do their job. Thus, while ISO neither accredits nor certifies, ISO standards define what counts as accreditation and enforcement and ISO works closely with similar international bodies that assure that similar standards for accreditation are used globally: ILAC (International Laboratory Accreditation Cooperation), founded in 1977, and the International Accreditation Forum (IAF) founded in 1993.[8]

Even if ISO itself has largely gotten out of the businesses of setting fundamental standards and of assessing the degree to which standards have been adhered to, it remains at the center of the global work that sets "product," "process," and "management systems standards." "Product standards" include, for example, specifying the size of shipping containers and the kind of corners that they must have so that they can be stacked easily. "Process standards" have to do with the conditions under which products and services are produced or generated; so, for example, ISO has issued standards for the training the women and men who oversee and operate the giant cranes that lift and transfer all those standard boxes.[9] Finally, "management systems standards," in ISO's words, "are often used to create a framework within which an organization consistently achieves the requirements set out in product and process standards."[10] As such, management systems standards have a great deal to do with questions of achieving conformity. ISO work in this third arena is the subject of the next chapter.

ISO documents describe the organization's product and process standards (our main concern in this chapter) as well as its support of fundamental standards, management systems standards, and conformity assessment all as contributing to fulfillment of human needs. They do so most directly, according to ISO's secretary general, Alan Bryden, by promoting economic growth through those two mechanisms discussed in Chapter 1: shaping innovation, or, in Bryden's words, "innovation and dissemination of new technologies," and encouraging the achievement of economies of scale and the benefits of comparative advantage that can be found in an ever freer, and increasingly global, market.[11]

ISO's role in encouraging the technologies that have created the *physical* infrastructure of today's global market illustrates both of these mechanisms, both of these ways in which ISO provides necessary *technical* infrastructure for the global economy. Therefore, in this chapter, we focus on the story of containerized shipping in part as an illustration of the ways in which ISO works to provide technical infrastructure aimed at shaping innovation and linking a larger market in many fields, and in part because standard setting relating to the physical infrastructure of shipping is the specific case in which ISO has, and continues to have, the greatest impact through these mechanisms. In contrast, in Chapter 5, when we turn to the "standards wars" in today's "information economy" we look at a case where ISO's role in shaping innovation and linking a global market has become more limited, while, in Chapter 4, we consider work that ISO officials see as contributing to "sustainable human development"—in more direct ways by encouraging "quality management" and by establishing environmental and social standards.

A standard and its consequences

In 1956, when the first container ship—a converted World War II oil tanker—left the dock in Newark, New Jersey, the world had neither the physical nor the technical infrastructure for a global consumer economy. Shipping costs were just too high.

It was not that the cost of moving a bunch of heavy objects across the oceans was, itself, prohibitive. Far from it: nature provided a normally smooth highway for free. The excessive costs had to do with packing and unpacking and loading and unloading any commodities that could not be shipped in bulk, the way oil or grains could be. In the 1950s, any manufactured product—in fact, anything other than some basic raw materials—was sent in a "break-bulk" ship that typically would be packed with 200,000 separate items: say, 70,000 cartons of mixed goods, 24,000 bags of papers and mail, 3,000 drums of different chemicals, 900 barrels of dishes, etc.[12] Each of the 200,000 items would have to be separately lifted into and out of the ship by crews of longshoremen. In the 1950s, port costs—the costs of all that movement in and out of the ship—made up over half the cost of sending cloth and clothes and most "Second Industrial Revolution" goods from an inland manufacturer on one continent to consumers on another. Such goods included medicines and other chemical products, electrical goods, and branded consumer products, which—together with the manufactured cloth and clothes of the original Industrial Revolution, make all the sorts of things one might find today in a US Wal-Mart or a French Carrefour.[13]

Before the container revolution, the cost of loading cargo into an average ship was US$5.86 per ton. Today, that cost is 16 cents.[14]

The proximate cause of this 93 percent reduction in cost was the publication, in 1965, of the ISO draft standards that define the most important parts of the containers that we see today—a metal box, eight feet wide and about eight feet high, usually 20 or 40 feet long, with doors at one end and reinforced corners that allow it to be clamped to other containers and to be stacked. Between 1956 and 1965, a tiny group of companies converted a few small ships to proprietary containers, but in the years immediately after the publication

Number of ships

Equivalent of 20-foot containers

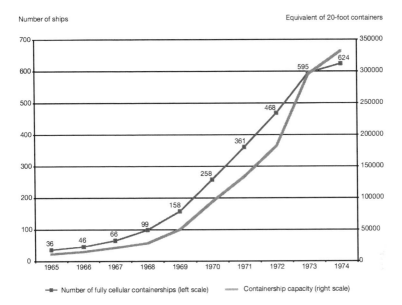

Figure 3.1 Containerships take off.
Source: UNCTAD, *Review of Maritime Transport*, 1973-4, 146.

of the standard, the building of ever-larger ships for the sole purpose of carrying ISO standard containers, took off (Figure 3.1).

Both the growing number of ships and their increasing capacity are equally important. The combined capacity of the approximately 600 containerships that were built in the first decade of the boom (by the mid-1970s) is the about the same as the combined capacity of three "super containerships" launched in 2007 and 2008, each of which can hold 11,000 to 12,000 of the standard containers.[15]

One historian of this change, Hugo van Driel, calls it, quite aptly, a "transportation revolution."[16] Yet, when containerization began, the revolutionary implications of shipping in standard boxes were far from fully recognized. In 1967, proponents estimated that perhaps, one day, 75 percent of the general cargo shipped across the North Atlantic could be transported in containers,[17] and, by 1995, the growing containerized proportion of the tonnage of general goods handled by Europe's largest port (Rotterdam) reached that level. The proportion has continued to grow. What is more important is that the cost savings from containerization have allowed the total tonnage of general goods through Rotterdam to increase tenfold in just 40 years.[18] Globally, container traffic continues to grow 10–15 percent each year, outstripping the growth rates of even the fastest growing economies, such as China.[19] Of course, the 13 percent average annual growth in container shipping over the last two decades was one of the key factors that allowed China's 9 percent average annual growth rate over the same period. John Fossey, a shipping industry observer, says that the container revolution explains, "[W]hy a person in Northern Europe who wants to eat strawberries on Christmas day can find them in their supermarket"; more generally, the revolution has been "a key enabler of the rapid industrialization and globalization we are seeing in the world today."[20]

The container revolution also transformed the landscape in many parts of the world, as well as the day-to-day working lives of millions of people. Container shipping caused some ports, such as Rotterdam, to grow, while others shrank. In the United States, it turned the once secondary ports of Long Beach, Newark, and Oakland into the sluiceways through which consumer goods flooded the country, and the revolution helped turn Singapore from a provincial backwater of the British Empire of the 1950s, a city where tigers were said to roam at the swampy edge, into the wealthy—if, sadly, tiger-free—model city-state of today.[21]

The change in the landscape was deeply connected to the change in working lives. Much of the 93 percent cost reduction that came with the container revolution was the result of savings in labor. In Britain's older ports, including London, labor resisted the new technology. Because the Transport and General Workers Union had never bothered to sign up workers in the tiny port of Felixstowe, it is now Britain's largest homeport. That is where investors moved, leaving London's impoverished docks empty, until the arrival of trendy young condo dwellers a generation later.[22]

In the US, the transformation of the docks involved buying out longshoremen with generous early retirement benefits. Eric Hoffer, the longshoreman-philosopher, an American cultural icon of the 1960s, complained, "This generation has no right to give away or to sell for money, [working] conditions that were handed to us by a previous generation," but his argument proved unpersuasive to fellow union members who welcomed the fat settlement.[23] One economist argues that this was an important real-world case that defies the prediction of the type of economics that has been popular since Thatcher and Reagan: the prediction that all "excess returns" will go to capital.[24] In fact, more generally, despite the pressure from containerization to reduce wages—both in ports and on ships—there has been no global "race to the bottom" that would have sent labor standards in shipping to ever lower levels. Instead, a diversity of different conditions continues to persist in different ports.[25]

Of course, the changes in the landscape and the changes in working lives did not end at the ports themselves. One of our friends who was a young man in the years after the oil price booms of the 1970s regaled us with stories of working one summer for a US office supply company that had him oversee the shipment of hundreds of containers of office equipment—desks, chairs, file cabinets, shelves, typewriters, calculators, and even those new-fangled coffee makers—to all the companies starting up business in Saudi Arabia's burgeoning economy. He accompanied the containers as they traveled across the ocean to Jeddah's sleek new port where massive new quay cranes lifted all the containers down to dock in just a few minutes and the technological marvel of a "straddle carrier"—a sort of massive forklift that can move a whole container— quickly ran up and placed them end to end along the dusty road to Riyadh. And there they sat for months, waiting for the new trucks and the necessary road improvements.[26]

The BBC's Toby Poston points to the global pattern that began with all the new roads and rail lines connecting to the container ports, "Manufacturers no longer had to crowd near ports or customers in order to reduce their transport costs. They could source cheaper components or even outsource production overseas as lower transport costs helped extend supply chains ... [D]eveloping nations were able to become suppliers to wealthier countries on the other side of the world."[27]

That meant prosperity, for some at least, in the developing world, and it is for that reason that ISO's champions talk about the container revolution as a major example of ISO contribution to sustainable human development. Nevertheless, the revolution meant hardship for others, especially some in North America and Western Europe. The new global economy undermined the mass-production and mass-consumption economies that had developed after the Second World War. As labor economist Stephen Herzenberg argues, "In retrospect, this seems inevitable given the way mass production designed production worker jobs to require minimal formal education and on-the-job training. Advances in telecommunications and reductions in transportation costs have made it possible for developing countries to approach advanced country productivity levels in mass-production operations."[28]

Setting the standard

Yet, even the briefest glance back at the history of containerized shipping reveals that the massive reductions in transportation costs were far from inevitable. Recall the argument of the contemporary French

standard setter, Jean-Daniel Merlet, that there is a "triangular" relationship among standardization, regulation, and innovation, in which
the regulatory environment often shapes efforts at standardization,
which, in turn, can enable or constrain different forms of innovation.[29]

Tineke Egyedi, who has looked at the history of container standards
in great depth, points out that standardization can play a particularly
transformative role (for good or for ill) when it, "facilitate[s] change in
large technical systems. More specific[ally], the flexibility, which is
required for system innovation, lies in the standardisation of *gateway
technologies*, [technologies that effectuate] whatever technical connections between distinct production sub-systems are required in order for
them to be utilized in conjunction, within a larger integrated production system."[30] The standardized container, Egyedi argues, is a quintes-
sential gateway technology. It is "a gateway between different subsystems
of transportation" that enhances the "efficiency of the system as a
whole."[31]

This "gateway" had been envisioned for decades before the work of
an ISO technical committee, TC-104, finally made it possible. Yet, ISO's
work was only a proximate cause of the transportation revolution. Before
there was any incentive to create a standard, the regulatory environment
had to change. In the USA, for example, the Interstate Commerce
Commission (ICC), the body that had regulated the cost of shipping
freight along the railroads from the 1880s onward, required that different
rates be charged for the same weight of different commodities; more
expensive commodities cost more to ship. When railroads tried to experiment with containers, the ICC ruled that they had to charge customers
for the entire container at the rate that applied to the most expensive
commodity in the container, even though the ICC "found the container to
be 'a commendable piece of equipment'" and recognized that its rules
assured that containers would "no longer make economic sense."[32]

By the 1950s, when US *ocean* shippers (definitely *not* railroads) finally
began to make investments in containers, and when some US regulators
began to desire the lower costs that a transformed global transportation infrastructure could provide, the pressure to gain agreement on
standards for this gateway technology increased dramatically. Yet, the
story of the ISO container is not just a story about the power of the
United States, and it is certainly *not* a story of the power of US companies *over* others, even though it is, in part, a story about the power of
US companies *to do* things that they believed were in their long-term
interests, at the cost of some shorter-term investments.

The container story is a major leitmotiv in the personal stories of
many leaders in the standards movement after the Second World War.

For example, Olle Sturén, the long-serving ISO secretary general, led the Swedish delegation to the first ISO meeting on container standards in 1959—one of his first forays into global standard setting[33]—and the Swedish records of those meetings are one of the few sets of technical committee documents maintained from the beginning with their historical significance in mind. Similarly, the American standard setter, Vince Grey, who eventually played a major role in ISO's early work on

---

Box 3.1   Finding ISO records

The work of technical committees has had a major impact on the global economy, yet it has been little studied, in part, because the records are hard to come by, largely because standards work is so widely distributed. Scholars who go to Geneva and ask to see the ISO archives are told that, because work is organized by the voluntary secretariats of the technical committees, there are no central archives; records are with the member bodies. Historians hear the same thing at the next level down, for example, the American National Standards Institute (ANSI) directs you to the trade associations or professional organizations that provided secretariats for its various the technical committees.

Because almost everyone involved in the standards business is quite gracious, we were eventually led to important records that had been kept—but not catalogued or maintained in archival conditions—at ISO and ANSI headquarters. Nonetheless, the experience of the scholars who have done the major studies of container standard setting is typical. Tineke M. Egyedi used the files of Swedish engineers who had been participants in many of the meetings and Marc Levinson gained his information from records that "may not be available in public archives."

Levinson comments, "[I]t's probably better for history that these records were not deposited with historians. They are in the hands of engineers, who are trained to keep everything in perfect order and never to throw anything out. So they are neatly filed away just as they were filed away in 1958!"

Sources: Marc Levinson, personal communication and *The Box: How the Shipping Container Made the World Smaller and the World Economy Bigger* (Princeton, N.J.: Princeton University Press, 2006), 312; Tineke M. Egyedi, "The Standardised Container: Gateway Technologies in Cargo Transport," *Homo Oeconomicus* 17, no. 3 (2000): 233.

information technology, was regularly called upon by the organization to explain how he, and ISO, moved from focusing on ships and marine technology to playing a role in every aspect of the global economy of the last decade.[34]

Grey was a US Merchant Marine engineering officer who entered graduate school in 1952 and at the same time took a job with the American Standards Association (ASA, as today's ANSI, the American National Standards Institute, was then known) where he got a taste of ISO standard setting as a US representative on ISO technical committees. After a short stint in the Navy, Grey arrived back at ASA in 1956, at just about the same moment that the first container ship left Newark harbor.[35]

Within a few month, two US companies, Matson and Sea-Land, had become the major competitors in the new trans-oceanic container shipping business, but their containers were incompatible and neither company envisioned a competitive, integrated intermodal system that could transfer boxes among the trucks, the railroad cars, the barges, and the ships owned by any company. However, businesses in many fields did envision such a system so, by the end of 1957, ASA had put together a huge (75-member) technical committee and was urging ISO to do the same.[36]

Initially, ASA was not the only American standard setter. The US government agencies that regulated ocean shipping and subsidized the building of US ships also wanted a standard. Ironically, because neither Sea-Land nor Matson were seeking subsidies, the US regulators did not consult them. The ocean shippers were part of the ASA process, but that process was dominated by container manufacturers, truckers, and railroads, who wanted to reach an agreement as rapidly as possible.[37]

Most accounts of the process agree that the chair of the ASA process, a retired Aluminum Company of America engineer, Herbert Hall, played the decisive role in getting agreement on the sizes of containers, including the most contentious issue of length. Hall was fascinated by what he called "preferred numbers," arguing for 10-, 20-, and 40-foot standard lengths. A shipper could use the appropriate size for a particular customer, but, because two of the small containers would fit in the space of the next larger container, the problem of packing them on ships would be minimized. By late 1959, ASA had a proposed US standard that it sent forward to ISO's TC-104 as a working document.[38]

Hall's 1959 standard meant that latecomers to containerization would be favored. Matson and Sea-Land, on the other hand, would have to write off tens of millions of dollars of recent investment. Yet, it was clear that if they did not accept the standard, they would lose US government contracts and would never be able to apply for subsidies, a point that was made clear immediately when the American Hawaiian Steamship Company was turned down for US federal mortgage insurance on a planned ship that would not accommodate the new standard containers.[39]

Not surprisingly, Matson and Sea-Land tried to change the ASA standard, but Hall, who continued to chair the committee for many years, persisted in his ruling that only the multiples of 10 feet had received sufficient support, including that of the US government agencies represented on the committee.[40] The companies then turned to Congress, which acquiesced to them in 1965 by amending the Merchant Marine Act so that no preference was given to firms following the ASA standard.[41]

However, by that point it was too late. The ISO process had greatly strengthened the ASA standard. Unlike ASA, ISO concentrated on "performance standards," on what containers should do rather than on how they should be constructed. That meant ISO could avoid long debates about the different benefits of aluminum (the favorite material in the US) versus steel (more popular in the rest of the world). It also meant that ISO had to face, head-on, one of the problems that still plagued the US standard, that of corner fittings and corner locks, the bits that "provide the place where the container is lifted and where it is secured during transport."[42]

A major breakthrough on this subject had been made in 1963, when Sea-Land, despite its anger over ASA's decision on standard sizes, released its patent rights to the corner fittings that were working successfully on the world's largest fleet of carriers. This example of the collective spirit that sometimes animates voluntary consensus standard setting proved decisive, but it was by no means unique. A sequence of events played into Sea-Land's decision. Two years earlier, the designer of the Sea-Land fitting had offered royalty-free use of a more recent fitting he had designed for one of Sea-Land's competitors, Fruehauf, for whom he was now chief engineer. Although, the Fruehauf design had not been proven in use, Fruehauf's example—and the desire for a common technology that would stimulate the growth of the industry— convinced Sea-Land to give up its own intellectual property.[43]

Nevertheless, even though the Sea-Land corners had proved adequate in many months of trans-oceanic shipping, they had not been tested under all of the conditions that would exist in a global intermodal transportation system. Part of ISO's job was to set up tests that simulate conditions in every part of the world, on railways bouncing down Swiss mountains or trucks in India's weaving stop-and-go traffic.

Vince Grey writes about a key 1965 ISO meeting in The Hague that agreed upon the test criteria and then waited as the American standard fittings were tested by a lab in Detroit, "How did the container do? Did it survive?" Unfortunately, no. The American standard was not adequate to take the loads that a container would experience in a worldwide intermodal system.[44] The Sea-Land corner would have to be further redesigned. "So," Grey recounts,

> we spun off a committee. We created an ad hoc committee to design a corner fitting with greater strength in whatever areas were needed so that it would pass the test. It was probably one of the most expensive sets of drawings that have ever been prepared in ISO. In that ad hoc committee, there were the Executive Vice-Presidents of these major companies, and they sat at a drafting board and drew these drawings. The ad hoc committee came back with its work and it was adopted ... for the next year containers were ordered and the purchase specification said "the corner fitting shall be the ad hoc committee corner fitting."[45]

It was after this Hague meeting that the container revolution took off. Yet, Grey adds, it took another two years, after a meeting in London, before, "someone could really go out in the manufacturing field and say, 'I want an ISO container.' We had a set of different documents which, when assembled, defined what is today 95% of the population of containers—a standard box, you know, with doors at one end and a closed roof."[46]

The final step before the ISO standard involved another set of emergency tests of the 1965 corner fitting, which had sometimes failed under heavy loads. Another ad hoc committee set up new tests and a British and a US engineer were sent off to a London "hotel room with their slide rules and told to redesign the fitting." Over the "bitter" objections of the many shipping companies that had had no problems with the 1965 standard, ISO approved the strengthened standard in a second 1967 meeting (this one in Moscow), even though the amendment required container owners to spend millions of dollars welding new fittings on the thousands of boxes that were only a few months old.[47]

Along the way to achieving the 1967 agreement, TC-104 also approved many ad hoc, and seemingly pointless, standards. It approved a special set of "alternative standard" boxes that happened to be the size of the few containers in the Eastern European trading area created by the Soviet Union. These boxes disappeared about as rapidly as Sea-Land and Matson's non-conforming boxes did. Similarly, ISO created an additional set of "alternative standard" boxes that were similar to those used on the railways of Western Europe. These boxes, too, disappeared. Grey comments, that, as a result, several ISO meetings later, TC-104 agreed to drop the alternatives. "That was the most tactful way to let something like that happen! It's better to get on with the work as long as you can achieve the basic goal and let the merits ... be judged by the users."[48]

In fact, *intra*-continental transport within Europe has evolved a set of what are called "swap bodies" that can be loaded with pallets and shifted from trucks to trains. They are containers that do not correspond to the ISO standards for global, intermodal transportation. Swap bodies are squat and wide; they allow relatively small packets of goods, mounted on pallets, to be moved in and out of the box by traditional forklifts. In that sense, these special European boxes are particularly appropriate to the shipment of small quantities of goods to their final destination, but they are not appropriate to the intercontinental shipment of the larger quantity of goods that could fill a whole container.

Egyedi comments that the economic contribution of ISO's improvements in intercontinental transport to European land transport is modest.[49] Fuel costs and the inefficiencies of the slow and winding paths needed to avoid natural obstacles and human settlement are largely what assure that the cost of shipping a container from China to Felixstowe is less than that for sending it the remaining 600 kilometers to Scotland.[50] Nevertheless, Egyedi argues that the "alternative gateway" that has evolved within Europe, the swap body, "corroded the potential of the ISO container as the unquestioned gateway for intermodal transport."[51]

Of course, the swap body exception to the global ISO container system reflects the fact that ISO standards are voluntary. European transport companies, especially state owned railroads, had the power to resist losing business to ISO standard truckers and to resist having to write off some of their fixed investments. They were able to convince European regulators and the European standard setting body to create the conditions that would preserve this alternative gateway.[52]

It is worthwhile to consider the other groups that did or did not seem to have similar power in the process of creating and maintaining the ISO standard. The advocates of other container sizes seem to have little power; the Eastern and Western European makers of alternative container sizes lost out to the market. Perhaps surprisingly, the companies with the major investments in containers of other sizes, Matson and Sea-Land, not only failed to prevail (even after turning to the US Congress), but Sea-Land even contributed its intellectual property to the standard that would eventually require the company to write off so much of its original investment. Grey argues that the result, "was not a willful effort to isolate the two pioneering companies, but was the result of broadening the scope of operations within which the containers would have to survive."[53]

That is true, perhaps, of ISO's strengthening of the component parts of the container, but it is not true relative to the question of size. More than anything else, the 10-foot "preferred numbers" reflected the engineering aesthetic of Herbert Hall, the chair of the ASA process who went on to take a leading role in ISO. Grey, who Hall had introduced to container standards in 1956 and who then worked for 35 years in the business—first as the secretary of TC-104, then as head of the US delegation, and then as chair of the technical committee for 15 years—retained Hall's conviction that a committee chair *should* propose such solutions, as long as he could do so "without showing favoritism to anyone."[54]

Recall from Chapter 2 (pages 39–40), that one prominent explanation of the success of the voluntary consensus standard setting mechanism emphasizes that many conflicts over standards represent "coordination problems" or "derived coordination problems" that can be solved by an authoritatively stated, but not necessarily "optimal," solution, a solution like the one suggested by Hall.

Another, compatible, explanation emphasizes the role of the technical committee as an institution with the "secret strengths" of "communicative rationality—the outcome of open discussion between equal individuals with different backgrounds."[55] Such discussion often leads individuals to focus on the long-term rather than the short-term, and to consider more collective goals rather than only personal or corporate goals. The agreements to give up intellectual property rights in order to facilitate the development of a standard reflect that kind of change in perspective. Moreover, ISO rules, especially the rule that national bodies are expected to represent all stakeholders, yet, at the same time, speak with a single voice, encourages members of technical committees to think of themselves as public trustees and not just as the representatives of their companies.

To maintain "open discussion between equal individuals with different backgrounds" often requires going out of one's way to maintain the sense of equality, which TC-104 did in approving the "alternate" standards desired by the Eastern and Western Europeans, in part as a kind of face-saving device for the regional standard setters. Similarly, such discussions require chairs who truly act "without showing favoritism to anyone."

Nonetheless, even though the companies that were the first movers into containerized shipping took an active and constructive part in a process of creating a standard that would be costly to them, after the ISO standard was set, Matson and Sea-Land certainly complained about it, and sought (and temporarily received) an exemption from the US rules that would make the standard obligatory.

Others complained about the ISO standard, as well. In particular, the governments of developing nations, working through the United Nations, attempted to establish an authoritative code, an intergovernmental treaty, that would protect the investments that a few developing nations had made in smaller containers before the ISO standard had been set.[56]

In addition, many of the rulers of the new nations in Africa and Asia were convinced that colonial monopolies over shipping to and from their countries had played a major role in their economic exploitation. This was, for example, a central argument in Kwame Nkrumah's *Neo-Colonialism*.[57] It probably did not help the ISO process that Nkrumah's democratically elected government was overthrown by a US and British-backed military coup in 1966, right in the middle of the final year of ISO container negotiations. This may have added to the bad impression of what Egyedi calls the "procedural *faux pas* of TC-104 (i.e. TC-104 meetings were exclusively held in industrial countries and experts, which drafted container standards, also came from these countries)."[58]

The objections of the developing world receded as the container revolution took off. This was, no doubt, in part because many Asian countries (and some African, Caribbean, and Latin American countries) gained so much from the trading opportunities that resulted. In addition, due to Olle Sturén's formative experience with the UN in the developing world, his tenure as secretary general of ISO—which began shortly after the first container standards were set—was marked by an active program of reaching out to the developing world. In 1972, Sturén convinced Robert Oteng, the head of Ghana's member body, to join the Geneva secretariat to "smooth out" difficulties with the developing world and establish a system of technical assistance to build the capacity of Third World standard setting bodies.[59] Nonetheless, as Chapter 4 illustrates, the legitimacy problem created by the lack of active Third World involvement in standard setting continued to plague ISO as it moved into the new fields of standards for quality management and social responsibility.

Certainly, the voices of some interested parties were amplified, and those of other interested parties were muffled, in the negotiations that led to ISO's container standards. That is true in the work of any

voluntary consensus standard setting body. If the voices of the technological first movers and the governments of the Third World were
muffled, that of the US government was amplified—at least at those
times when the US government spoke with one voice! The United
States had a strong interest in a global container standard, both as a
customer that shipped a great deal to its growing network of military
bases in Europe, Asia, and the Pacific, and as provider of subsidies to
the US shipping industry. The US government played a key role in
pushing the standard setting process at the beginning, and that proved
decisive. Congress's later attempt to ease, temporarily, the US government's pressure in favor of the ISO standard (in response to Matson
and Sea-Land's complaints) had little effect. The ISO standard encouraged a new industry that supplanted the system of proprietary containers that developed in the late 1950s; after 1965, "[l]easing companies
began to feel confident investing large sums in containers and moved
into the field in a big way." Most shippers wanted the flexibility that
could come from renting, rather than owning, most of the containers
that they used and the leasing companies were interested in providing
only one kind of box.[60]

After ISO set the standard, the market and the state continued to
reinforce it. Most manufacturers wanted to be able to fill a container at
any factory in the world and know "with a high degree of confidence
that almost any trucks, trains, ports, and ships would be able to move it
smoothly all the way" to any purchaser anywhere else.[61] Governments,
in their role as major purchasers, reinforced the standard. They also
did so in their roles as major financiers, builders, and operators of
ports, and, occasionally, as regulators of those ports, and of roads and
railroads.[62] Yet, it is unlikely that either governments, or the market, or
governments and the market together would have been able to trigger
the transportation revolution without the voluntary consensus standard
setters.

Other physical infrastructure, technical infrastructure, and conformance

ISO's involvement with the container revolution did not end with the
agreement on the standard box. The persistence and extent of ISO's
involvement can be gauged by imagining the movements of a typical
container both before and after that moment when it is about to be
lifted off a ship. With those sequences in mind, we can search through
the ISO standards catalogue.[63] "Containers" brings up over 100 standards, including ISO 1496-2–Specification and testing of thermal

containers, last revised in 1996. "Cranes" gives another 100, including the 2003 update of ISO 4306–Cranes–vocabulary. Standards for "road vehicles" include another 2003 standard that is relevant to trucks that trail two or three ISO containers mounted on wheels: ISO 4901– Connections for the electrical connection of towing and towed vehicles. The violent shaking that broke the ASA corner fitting when they were subjected to a simulation of European "railways" is the subject of 2005's ISO 2017–Technical information to be exchanged for the application of vibration isolation associated with railway systems. Ships themselves are the subject of scores of standards, including the 2004 ISO15749–Drainage systems on ships and maritime structures, while "warehouses" takes you to a set of standards reworked shortly after the container revolution began, for example, ISO 2633–Determination of imposed floor loads in production buildings and warehouses, completed in 1974.

Given both the growing demand for containers and the limited supply of one of their parts—their internal wood floors—it is likely that ISO will be busy over the next decade in setting standards for bamboo-floored containers, and the entire bamboo plywood industry. As one Chinese forest products engineer told the UN Food and Agricultural Agency, in 1995, as his country's exports increase, "so will demand for container floorboards. Since few plywood plants can produce container floorboards, China is presently importing a large quantity and sometimes has difficulties regarding the continuity of supply. This confirms the urgent need to develop the bamboo container floorboard industry."[64] In 2007, the industry had taken off, but there were no standards to assure that the bamboo in the floors was being grown sustainably and that the plywood was made in a non-toxic manner.[65]

ISO is not just concerned with standardizing key bits and pieces of the physical infrastructure of the global trading area; it is equally concerned with contributing to other parts of technical infrastructure of the global economy. It is still deeply concerned with setting the standards for metrology, or "fundamental standards," that are administered by other organizations. For example, these days, many of those containers crossing the oceans are filled with little bottles of drinking water; we can buy water from Fiji, France, Iceland, and New Zealand in the nearest convenience store to our house in a largely working-class suburb of Boston. The industry may be socially and environmentally absurd, but it is probably not going to kill anyone, in part due to new standards for testing water quality that ISO has promulgated. However, those standards, in turn, have required new fundamental standards for measuring some of the basic characteristics of water, such as ISO 10703–Water quality–Determination of the active concentration of radionuclides.

ISO standards also facilitate the control systems that help move goods rapidly from place to place. ISO codes identify and mark over 90 percent of the containers shipped around the world. These codes and markings, in combination with shipping documents, which ISO also helps to standardize, make it possible for shipping to be done without opening and reopening containers in order to inspect their contents as they cross borders.[66]

These control systems for goods in transit—the documents and markings—would be totally ineffective if there were no way to assure that containers remained sealed while in transit. Again, ISO provides a number of standards for electronic and conventional seals that are applied to most containers.[67]

This only leaves some questions about what goes into the containers in the first place. Governments, and various private standard setting bodies, have developed codes for monitoring the packing of containers. In part, this is because the governments of most countries regulate the export of certain goods and the governments of some countries in the developing world have systems of export duties or licenses. Another major concern, especially in the wake of the September 2001 terrorist attacks in the United States, comes from wealthy countries receiving containers from the developing world; it is widely believed that terrorists might try to use poorly guarded containers to deliver weapons of mass destruction.[68] One of the fields in which ISO recently has been developing standards the most rapidly involves so-called "supply chain security," a major focus of TC-8 Ships and marine technology.[69]

One part of the "conformance assessment industry," which has burgeoned with the current wave of globalization, is concerned with verifying what gets packed into shipping containers. In fact, some of the major national standards bodies have gotten into that business in a big way. In 1998, BSI (the British Standards Institute) purchased a major multinational in the field, a firm called "Inspectorate" that provides independent inspection, analysis, and testing of cargoes. Much of its work is in "developing countries and often with complex local arrangements about tariffs and subsidies. Its role is to inspect pre-shipment cargoes (which can be of almost any type of product) to establish conformity to contract or to ensure that import and export transactions are above board and comply with local regulations."[70]

BSI sold Inspectorate in 2005, in a move that reflected some of the current confusion over what the boundaries should be among the worlds' standard setters, conformance assessors, and accreditation agencies.[71] Nonetheless, there is some irony to the fact that, for a short period of time, one could have argued that the "agency of global governance" that did the most to assure that terrorists could not sneak weapons of mass destruction into major ports was just a division of the oldest of the voluntary consensus standards agencies.[72] When, a century before, Sidney and Beatrice Webb had written about the need for the "further development" of BSI's "impossible to over-rate" activities, this is undoubtedly *not* what they had in mind.[73]

Conformance with more prosaic standards is equally important to the global trading area that has been linked by the container revolution. Like the water quality standards that help make it possible for there to be bottled water from Fiji in a Boston-area convenience store, most ISO standards still refer to kinds and grades of materials and manufactured goods, as well as to expectations about the performance of those goods and commodities. In addition, over 1,000 of ISO's published standards define standard procedures for testing products to assure that they meet those standards for everything from the rate at which a specific grade of steel will corrode to the tolerances that should be allowed in the machines that test the machines that test the flexibility of artificial knees![74]

For global trade to work efficiently, it is extremely helpful if the tests about conformance to such standards can be done at the point at which the items are manufactured, rather than at the point at which they are used. It is one thing if a French surgeon finds a stale croissant at the corner patisserie; it is another thing if she finds a defective artificial knee made by a plant in China. It would be a bit more of a bother to her, and to her patient, if she had to send the knee back. The same would be true of a builder in South Africa who tests and finds that a steel beam from Korea corrodes more rapidly than it should.

The demands of efficiency have created a global need for more organizations (public and private) to perform conformity assessment in all parts of the world. ISO sets standards for the bodies that do conformity assessment; the ISO/IEC 17000 series of standards defines terms and sets out standards for impartiality and confidentiality as well as a grievance procedure. It also establishes the criteria for the bodies that give accreditation to the organizations that test for conformance.[75]

Applying these standards, watching over the entire accreditation and conformance business, is a group of national accreditation bodies, almost all of which have very close connections to the national standard setting bodies that are part of ISO. Thus, for example, the US body, the ANSI-ASQ National Accreditation Board (ANAB), is a joint venture, begun in 2005, of ANSI and the American Society for Quality, a professional society in the quality management field,[76] while the influential Joint Accreditation System of Australia and New Zealand grew from an entrepreneurial push by Standards Australia.[77] In some cases, including Canada and Malaysia, the accreditation body and the national standards body are one and the same.[78]

There is good reason for at least a formal separation between the national accreditation body and the ISO national member body that typifies most countries. The accreditation bodies are meant to give an objective assessment of the degree to which various "conformance certification bodies" live up to the international standards for such work, and, most national standards bodies now want to do that conformance work, so they cannot be in the business of accrediting themselves! In the case of Standards Australia, which went into the conformance assessment business in the late 1980s, the organization was transformed because it had "tapped into a huge new market." Winton Higgins writes, "[C]ontroversy over Standards Australia's commercial success began at this time, with the success itself, and was never to leave it."[79] BSI, which has also been successful in following a similar path, required a 1998 change in its Royal Charter to begin to pursue the business, but since that point it has acquired companies that are major providers of certification in Southeast Asia, Europe, North America, and "in order to consolidate the Group's penetration of the immense Greater China certification market."[80]

In 1993, the national accreditation bodies met to create a parallel global structure to ISO. The International Accreditation Forum (IAF), which is based in Australia, brings together the world's conformity assessment and accreditation organizations in the same way that ISO brings together the organizations that set the standards in the first place. IAF's major purpose is to assure that companies and governments seeking conformity assessments will treat the work of all "accredited assessors" in the same way.[81] On the one hand, this means that (say) a builder in South Africa will be confident in the assessment of the steel given by any of a wide range of government agencies, private laboratories, or quasi-non-profit international companies (such as BSI) that his Korean supplier might employ. On the other hand, because IAF is made up of organizations closely related to national standard setting bodies that carry out the very profitable work of conformity assessment, some worry about the standards bodies becoming subjects of Adam Smith's observation, "People of the same trade seldom meet together ... but the conversation ends in a conspiracy against the public, or in some contrivance to raise prices."[82] As Higgins suggests, while it is certainly true that ISO and its members facilitated the transformations in infrastructure that led to contemporary globalization, some member bodies have also gained a great deal of business as a result!

Conclusion

ISO's current role in global governance was forged in the 1960s, when the organization began setting the standards for containerized shipping that help create global markets. Much of ISO's work that is more recent responds to the problems and opportunities created by that global market. The details of the original negotiations on container standards illustrate many of the characteristics that are common to almost all ISO standard setting: major industrialized countries played a central role in the process. The relevant companies were all at the table, but the major players did not necessarily get the standard they desired. Some companies were willing to give up proprietary knowledge in order to facilitate agreement. Moreover, engineering norms, and the persuasiveness of particular individuals, played a key role in the agreement.

The container case also illustrates how successful standard setting in one field can lead to whole range of new ISO activities in other fields. The shipping container enlarged—in fact, globalized—the world's major trading area, and ISO followed as the center of standard setting for goods and services in all fields. As the scope of ISO's work expanded, so did the opportunities for organizations and companies who certify that particular products conform to international standards, and to bodies that certify the certifiers. While ISO itself has not taken on these tasks, certification and accreditation have become important sources of revenue for some ISO member bodies, some of which have come to resemble extremely successful multinational firms. Taken as a whole, the entire network of voluntary consensus standard setting organizations now carries out a surprisingly wide range of tasks of global governance, even including security tasks as well as the social and environmental regulation that is the topic of the next chapter.

4 From quality management to social regulation

Conformance assessment has turned many national standards bodies into profitable businesses—into organizations that look as much like multinational corporations as they do like NGOs (non-governmental organizations) or the constituent parts of the United Nations (UN) system. The greatest spur to the expanding business of conformance assessment has been ISO's publication, in 1987, of a quality management standard, ISO 9000. ISO's experience with that standard, has, for the first time, given the organization the desire and the capacity to take on a much broader agenda of social regulation. Therefore, somewhat paradoxically, at the very moment at which some observers have begun to worry that key voluntary standard setting bodies have lost their "secret strength"—their immersion in a "civic culture" that values much more than profit-making[1]—ISO has actually begun to become an alternative to our ineffective UN system of intergovernmental organization, a development that some observers of voluntary consensus standard setting have championed for almost a century.

Even if ISO could hardly be thought of as a replacement for the UN, through its work in environmental and social responsibility standards, ISO has begun to contribute, directly, to the goals of "sustainable human development" that it shares with the UN.

This chapter explores the origins of ISO 9000 and why it spread. We then turn to the links between this quality management standard and ISO's work on environmental standards and standards for corporate social responsibility (CSR). We link ISO's work to current debates about the UN's Global Compact and other global governance initiatives that rely on businesses and professional associations.

The chapter could have been entitled "Shaping Quality—Enhancing Competition" because that is how many of those who work with and within ISO conceive of the link between ISO 9000 and the later series of standards on the environment (ISO 14000) and social responsibility

(ISO 26000). Fundamental standards (like weights and measures) and product standards (ISO's original forte) shape competition by limiting some of the differences between similar products that different companies bring to the market: "better" product standards are those that convince companies to compete over features that matter most to consumers. The standards discussed in this chapter shape competition in a different way. "Quality management" standards are supposed to improve *all* of an organization's processes so that, over time, *all* of the features of *all* of its products will improve. Effective environmental standards, labor standards, and human rights standards push firms toward different overall business strategies, strategies that—again—enhance conditions that many people consider to be socially desirable *overall*.

Quality management standards and high social standards also tend to reinforce each other. Political economists Michael J. Piore[2] and Stephen Herzenberg[3] argue that improving global labor standards would tend to push businesses toward quality-enhancing types of competition because, in order to cover the costs associated with making improvements in labor conditions, companies would need to invest in improvements in labor productivity. Increased productivity would, in turn, tend to lead to higher-quality products because productivity gains would probably require improving workers' skills, which tends to reduce defects. Similarly, when a firm has invested in a quality management system, it is likely to invest in additional training and more general education for its workers. Those investments will be needed to give workers the capacity to use the new management system effectively, and those improvements in "human capital," in turn, are likely to lead to improvements in working conditions, even if only indirectly, simply because more skilled workers generally are able to make greater demands on their employers.

Of course, having organizations adopt ISO standards is far from the only way either to improve the quality of management or to better society more generally. The fields of social and economic development are concerned with the much broader range of techniques that are available. They include government programs to improve education and training (developing human capital), the adoption of model legal codes, encouraging the formation of a vibrant civil society (developing "social capital"), and the ratification of international treaties that lay out specific individual and collective rights. ISO standard setters simply argue that some international voluntary consensus standards can contribute to an environmentally sustainable form of such development.

This is a very different argument from the one that was used to justify ISO at its foundation: the argument that international standards help create the widest possible trading area in which regions and firms can find their comparative advantage.

A new focus begins: ISO 9000

Nonetheless, the traditional argument—the one about expanding opportunities for trade—was key to ISO's decision to enter into the quality management field in the 1980s. In addition, it is clear that most firms that adopt ISO 9000, especially those in the developing world, do so in order to increase their market. One team that has studied the impact of ISO 9000 in 140 countries puts it this way: "Spatial, cultural, and linguistic barriers create information asymmetries between buyers and sellers that impede international trade." ISO 9000 reduces "these information asymmetries by providing assurance of product quality by firms that receive its certification."[4]

ISO 9000 is closely linked to the most recent period of economic globalization that began after the container revolution in the 1970s. While there have been "off the shelf" quality management standards that firms could purchase and adopt since the 1950s, the growth in actual adoptions has been "explosive"—or at least exponential—since the mid-1990s, and the vast majority of recent adoptions have been of ISO standards and not those of ISO's competitors.[5] In 2001, there were 44,000 organizations around the world that had been certified as conforming to ISO's quality management standard. By 2005, the number had grown almost 20-fold to nearly 800,000—with little sign that the growth would abate any time soon.[6]

When an organization adopts a Quality Management System (QMS)—and it is such a system that is provided by the ISO standard—the organization makes a commitment to its primary clients (its "customers," if it is a firm selling some product) to focus on the client's goals, not to be distracted by other goals, to reflect continuously on everything the organization does with its client's concerns in mind, and to try constantly to improve on how well the organization does what it intends to do. The "customer orientation" of quality management can, in a subtle way, be quite radical; it provides an opening for a more "civic" view of the role of a corporation. This orientation requires that a private company tell itself, "Our mission is to create x or y product or service for this group of people," which is a very different from, "Our goal is to make the most profit that we can."

The compatibility of quality management with the goals of more "civic" organizations is one reason for the success of ISO 9000. In 2006, one commentator, reflecting on the explosive growth of the standard, marveled, "Who would have thought 20 years ago that financial institutions, schools, blood banks, prison systems, Buddhist temples, cruise lines, or retail chains would implement ISO 9001?"[7] Yet, the idea of "quality management" can apply to most organizations, not just to profit-making companies that want to boost sales to paying customers. In fact, many QMS principles are commonsense to many organizations that are quite different from commercial firms.

For example, a college or university might understand its fundamental goal as "preserving and extending the knowledge of our society." The educators might agree to stop doing anything that would distract them from that overarching goal, as when the University of Chicago's Robert M. Hutchins abolished the football program, declaring that it had "the same relation to education as bullfighting has to agriculture."[8] The school might set up systems for continuously monitoring its students' learning and its faculty's research. Finally, the university's leadership might institute systems of rewards for scholarly breakthroughs and for assuring that each entering class of students is able to learn more than those that came before it. None of these ideas would be strange to university professors in the sciences, or in any field in which knowledge seems to grow.

If a QMS can make an organization more effective at achieving its particular goals, that should be reason enough to adopt it. Commercial firms will be reminded of this by pressure of the market: if your competitors have adopted an effective QMS, you may have to do so as well, if only to signal that you, too, believe in quality. The "father" of quality management, US statistician W. Edwards Deming, used to say, "You don't *have* to do this. Survival is not compulsory."[9] Like other "voluntary" consensus standards, quality management may become a necessity.

Yet this might not be the whole explanation for the rapid adoption of ISO 9000. Critics argue that ISO's 9000 series (there are a group of standards that work together[10]) creates a relatively poor QMS, one that may be useful to some organizations, but that is less effective than other systems that are available. The critics point out that ISO 9000 includes its own somewhat cunning way of promoting its further adoption: The standard requires that organizations that are certified as ISO 9000 compliant must work only with suppliers and other "partners" who also have a QMS in place, and ISO 9000, while not the best system around, is the one that is the most readily available, and the most convincing proof to the bodies that certify conformance with the standard.[11]

To understand the criticism of ISO 9000 we need to go back to the beginning of the "quality management movement." This is another business-oriented social movement that, like the standardization movement itself, began in the early twentieth century.

A century ago, many leading sector firms experimented with new ways to use information to control and improve output. The US chemical company DuPont, for example, pioneered an innovative set of charts that traced the contribution of every aspect of production to the firm's ultimate return on investment.[12] In 1924, Walter Shewhart, a statistician working for the Western Electric Company, developed a different set of linked charts that recorded qualities of parts and product assemblages as they passed through different stages of production. The charts allowed managers and workers to identify, very rapidly, any unexpected variations that could lead to poor quality. One of Shewhart's main concerns was to distinguish those unexpected deviations from the random variations that one has to expect in any process. Shewhart's ideas were quickly adopted by his colleague, W. Edwards Deming, who soon entered the US government and eventually played an important role as a consultant to the occupying powers in Japan immediately after the Second World War.

Deming inspired a number of Japanese managers who wanted to establish a global reputation for Japanese products. By the late 1970s, with fears of Japanese competition growing among managers in the countries that had been the victors in the war, Deming began being treated as a forgotten prophet by many businessmen and government officials in Western Europe, the United States, Canada, Australia, and New Zealand.[13]

Like many prophets, Deming lost control of his message. When the idea of a QMS standard came to ISO in 1977, the fundamental image that most of its proponents had in mind was not Shewhart's charts that would allow *anyone* to quickly detect anything other than random variations at any stage of manufacturing. It was, instead, the *hierarchical* image of the military assuring "zero defects" in the manufacture of weaponry. As a prominent critic of ISO 9000 puts it,

> During World War 2 the UK's Ministry of Defence had a problem—bombs were going off in the factories. To solve the problem they based inspectors in factories that supplied munitions. If you wanted to be a supplier, you had to write down the procedures for making your product, you had to ensure that your workers worked to these procedures by inspecting their work and finally you had to have this whole method of working inspected by a Government inspector. From this seed, a whole forest of control and inspection has grown in the name of quality.[14]

The man who put quality management on ISO's agenda was a retired Canadian admiral, Ralph Hennessy, who had moved from the Navy in 1970 to become the first executive director of the Standards Council of Canada. In 1976, he became ISO vice president and chair of the agenda-setting Technical Management Board, where, working in cooperation with German, French, and British standard setters who were concerned about new fields that demanded "zero defects"—offshore drilling, nuclear power, and aerospace systems—he quickly established TC-176 Quality management and quality assurance.[15]

Discussions in TC-176 continued for many years and concluded with the adoption of a standard based on a British Standards Institute (BSI) model in 1987. Commentators attribute both the conclusion of the drawn-out discussion and the rapid adoption of the new standard to the concerns of many European governments that, without QMS, many of their national firms would be uncompetitive in the new, more open global economy that seemed desirable or, at least, inevitable. Digital Equipment Company executive, Robert Kennedy (a longtime TC-176 member) told Sun Microsystems' Carl F. Cargill that the new standard was

> Margaret Thatcher's way of trying to get several hundreds of thousands of small British firms ready to compete in the commerce of the Unified Europe and in the international arena. He pointed out that many small European firms who were soon to have to play in an expanded market, had no idea of what quality was national or internationally, nor how to achieve it.[16]

Historian Winton Higgins points to the similar pressures in Australia and New Zealand. Both countries had begun to open their domestic markets for manufactured goods in the 1980s and they needed something like ISO 9000 so that their own fusty old firms would learn how to compete.[17]

Yet, it is not clear that the original ISO 9000 did much beyond demanding that organizations have a "customer orientation" to assure that they would become more competitive. Most of the standard was concerned with documenting every part of an organization's operations, establishing measurable objectives for every process, and assuring some kind of corrective feedback if those objectives were not met. This was not necessarily the kind of system that would have been advocated by those with the most understanding of effective QMS at the time. Outside of those fields in which "zero defects" were critical, quality management experts tended to promote systems that gave everyone in the organization incentives to improve work processes at all levels.[18]

Cargill argues that, by itself, the ISO standard "doesn't produce quality; if you have a really well-administered program that produces trashy goods, you still will have a good [ISO 9000] program and not quality."[19] When ISO 9000 certifiers come to a company to determine whether the standard is in place, they basically ask: Are the organization's processes documented? Are the processes carried out the way the documents say they should be carried out? And, do the processes provide the expected results?[20] If, as Cargill suggests, all that management expects is trashy goods (which, unfortunately, might be all its customers expect, as well), the certifiers will just verify that the company has a well documented system that will assure such goods are made.

Hitoshi Kume, a leader in the Japanese QMS movement, argues that using quality control to assure continuous improvement is quite a different matter, one that requires the organization to focus on such improvement, and not simply on the "purchaser's requirements."[21] Other Japanese manufacturers worry about the somewhat perverse ways in which ISO 9000's goal of documenting everything underestimates the importance of the tacit knowledge that may allow almost any worker or manager to guess quite accurately about what may be causing an unexpected variation at any point in the production process. This is a significant advantage of most Japanese systems that was recognized in the management literature, but was ignored in the original ISO standard.[22]

The limitations of the original ISO QMS have led to a host of pop-culture references to the seeming busywork needed to conform to the standard (see Figure 4.1). One participant is such a system describes a typical experience: "The month before our factory was scheduled to have an ISO 9000 audit, we all spent days and nights filling in records.

Figure 4.1 Preparing for an ISO 9000 audit.
Source: DILBERT: © 1995 Scott Adams/Dist. by United Feature Syndicate, Inc.

Our factory passed the ISO 9000 audit! However, the records at the factory did not necessarily represent the practices on the shopfloor."[23]

Yet, some of the common criticisms of the ISO standard may be a bit misplaced. Cargill argues, "[I]t is not a great quality program, but it does provide a company that has only a vague idea about quality a starting point from which to build," which was largely the intent of those who set the standard in the first place.[24] Moreover, TC-176 has continuously updated the standard and even ISO 9000's severest critics acknowledge that it keeps moving further away from the top-down military standards out of which it grew, and closer to the kind of management system that one might find in firms with the greatest commitment to improving quality. Now, instead of disparaging ISO 9000, Japanese QMS consultants just write about the ways in which it needs to be implemented in order to be truly effective.[25]

Reflecting the same trend, official ISO texts keep rewriting the history of the standard to emphasize connections to Deming and quality management in Japan rather than to US, Canadian, and British military standards. This revisionism began relatively early on. In 1999, after recalling the "partisan" disputes about the standard's history, ISO secretary general Lawrence Eicher winked to a knowledgeable Canadian audience, "Whatever the origins, we know that ISO 9000 has become an international reference for quality requirements in business to business dealings."[26]

R. Dan Reid, one of the major standard setters for General Motors— perhaps the company that had lost the most to the success of quality management in Japan—points to how implementation of ISO 9000 standards has led to the harmonization of the supply chains of most major auto firms, and thus to great savings, but, perhaps more significantly, how familiarity with ISO 9000 led to the development of *new* quality standards that were of particular interest to automobile firms that were not part of the Japanese quality culture.[27] The standard which Reid was involved in setting, ISO/TS 16449:2002 Quality management systems–Particular requirements ... for automotive production and relevant service parts organizations, has been adopted by more than 17,000 firms primarily in the United States, China, Germany, India, and other countries where the industry did not have the Japanese experience with quality management.[28]

Even when adoption of ISO 9000 may not serve as the beginning of a process of learning how to do effective quality management, adoption can be beneficial. On the one hand, the costs of ISO 9000 are relatively low, and they vary dramatically depending on whether or not an organization already has a QMS in place. In the mid-1990s, a new

British university (a former polytechnic) with some 20,000 students that had no QMS in place—and which was quite unsure about the effectiveness of its traditional systems for continuous improvement—estimated that implementing ISO 9000 required the equivalent of 20 new administrative and clerical positions.[29] On the other hand, the average small or medium size Japanese firm, with a strong QMS in place, estimated their investment as "an average of $25,000 to $50,000 (including internal costs, consultations, and audits)."[30]

In Japan, that cost is largely an investment in signaling to customers, suppliers, investors, and regulators, around the world, that the firm really cares about quality management. According to German economist Cornelia Stortz, many Japanese managers report that "ISO 9000 is only an empty shell." Firms do not necessarily comply with everything it suggests. "As a result, ISO 9000 reaches only into management processes at the periphery, if at all, leaving the already existing quality management processes for the most part undisturbed."[31] Arguably, though, this is a *strength* of the voluntary standard: In many cases, it leaves a relatively strong quality culture undisturbed while providing an inexpensive way to communicate to outsiders that such a culture exists. In other cases, as with the US auto industry, it helps to establish such a culture in the first place.

The important signaling role that ISO 9000 plays explains the somewhat paradoxical empirical finding that, around the world, firms with a great deal of understanding and knowledge of quality management are more likely to adopt this less-than-perfect standard than are firms with little knowledge of quality management.[32] While the knowledgeable firms may be adopting ISO 9000 primarily as a way of letting others know about a long-standing commitment to quality management, there is another group of firms, largely in the already industrialized world, that adopted ISO 9000 as way to begin to put a more complex QMS in place. Many of these firms were convinced to adopt the standard due to the pressure of governments, especially the promotion of the standard by the British government and by the EU. Initially, the most important source of government influence has been its role as a large purchaser—a purchaser who required that suppliers have a QMS in place.[33]

Companies in the developing world have also been able to use ISO 9000 certification as a mechanism for signaling a commitment to quality and as a way of beginning to build a quality culture. The purchasing requirements of some EU governments seem to have provided some incentive for African, Asian, and Latin American companies to adopt the standard, but requirements of multinational firms appear to be even more important.[34] It is certainly clear that if firms in developing countries can comply with ISO 9000, they can enter some new markets and help pull their national economies up from the bottom of the supply chain. At the same time, as firms in developing countries gain more experience with ISO 9000, they are able to take a more active part in the formulation of related ISO standards, something that may increase the legitimacy of the environmental and social responsibility standards that have been built on the ISO 9000 base.[35]

Paradoxically, perhaps, the Japanese experience with ISO 9000 has led to a similar outcome of greater Japanese involvement in setting both ISO quality standards and standards that build upon them. Many Japanese companies and the Japanese popular and business press may find the ISO standard a bit offensive—a necessary cost of business, a way of signaling, globally, a much deeper, local, commitment to quality management—but the experience with the standard led to a new level of Japanese commitment to being involved in setting any similar standards created in the future. In the words of one Japanese business organization, the aim is, "to formulate world standards that start from Japan,"[36] a commitment that may help the larger program that ISO has built on its experience with quality management.

ISO 14000: From QMS to private regulation of environmental harms

ISO's first major attempt to build on its experience with creating management standards came in 1996 when it issued the first of the ISO 14000 standards. The ISO 14000 series of standards defines an "Environmental Management System" (EMS) that includes a certification standard (ISO 14001) and includes standards on environmental labeling, life cycles assessment (monitoring what happens to materials throughout the production process, use, and disposal), and even the management of greenhouse gas emissions. As with ISO 9000, much of the explosion of ISO 14000 certifications took place at the beginning of the twenty-first century. In 2001, some 36,000 organizations, globally, had passed ISO 14001 certification. By 2005, the number had tripled to 111,000. The two countries with by far the most certifications were Japan (nearly 25,000) and China (about half as many).[37]

ISO's interest in establishing environmental standards goes back to the 1960s; it was one of the emergent issues that Olle Sturén identified when he became ISO's secretary general.[38] Yet, it took until the early 1990s before the organization focused a great deal of attention on the issue.

In part, ISO's interest in an EMS standard at this time was triggered by the fact that most existing environmental management systems employed many of the same principles as the 1987 ISO 9000 QMS standard; they involved identification of things that the organization wanted to avoid as it carried out its work, documentation of work processes, internal monitoring, and some system of feedback. Moreover, the kind of certification system that existed for ISO 9000 would, with very little modification, be useful for certifying the existence of a standard EMS.[39]

At the same time, again in the early 1990s, many private firms anticipated that they soon would be required, by governments or by their customers, to put some kind of EMS in place. In 1992, the UN sponsored the highly publicized "Earth Summit" at which almost all of the world's governments, under the pressure of the environmental movement, pledged to work together to combat climate change and the accelerating rate of extinctions and to promote environmentally sustainable development. The growing power of the environmental movement assured that such systems would become a requirement under the legislation of at least some countries. At the same time, the principles of the GATT (General Agreement on Tariffs and Trade) standards code—which were strengthened in 1995 when GATT became the World Trade Organization (WTO)—made it likely that conformance with an international voluntary EMS would prove just as acceptable to most governments, none of which had the capacity to actually inspect firms and enforce the tens of thousands of pages of environmental regulations that the most active governments had established. It was likely that firms would be able to maintain their access to the markets of even the most environmentally strict jurisdictions just by being certified as having conformed to an ISO standard.[40]

By 2005—a decade after the initial publication of ISO 14000—the weight of the accumulated evidence suggested that those firms adopting the standard were also complying more fully with existing environmental regulations than were otherwise similar firms. In addition, some relatively convincing evidence suggested real improvement in the adopters' environmental performance: The ISO 14000 firms polluted less than they had in the past, and less than their competitors did.[41] Moreover, one well designed study indicated that the desire of firms to get into markets where ISO 14000 was an important voluntary supplement to, or substitute for, strong environmental regulation was fueling the rapid adoption of the standard around the world.[42]

The studies done so far suggest that the effectiveness of the standard is connected to the fact that there are "third parties"—the conformance certifiers—who provide a kind of public disclosure of firm practices. Because that information exists, consumers, environmental NGOs, and, of course, government regulators are able to isolate those organizations that fail to improve their environmental performance. Some commentators have, therefore, called corporate disclosure of information—transparency—the fundamental principle of effective global environmental governance.[43] Political scientists Aseem Prakash and Matthew Potoski argue that the "adversary legalism" that characterizes the political system in the United States makes firms reluctant to become so transparent, which is, they believe one of the reasons that ISO 14000 has not been as widely adopted by US firms.[44]

Prakash and Potoski see ISO 14000 as a mechanism for husbanding the coercive power of the state, consumers, and NGOs. It is, they believe, a simple "rational choice" mechanism for solving a collective action problem, a way of assuring that organizations do not create "negative environmental externalities," which, they believe, all organizations will do unless they face some greater disincentive.[45]

Yet, ISO also tries to solve this collective action problem by building on the *identity*—the positive commitment to a larger social good rather than to mere profit maximization—that many organizations have reinforced through involvement in ISO 9000. Firms committed to quality management, ISO argues, simply do not want to produce negative environmental externalities. At the beginning of a film introducing ISO 14000, the cheery announcer says, "It is easy to agree that organizations should reduce to a minimum any harmful effects of their activities on the environment."[46] Prakash and Potoski and other observers committed to a rational choice framework would not agree. Yet, perhaps it *is* easy: If your organization is committed to quality management—if it has a calling to provide the best to some group of clients—then perhaps adopting an effective EMS will seem just as obvious as dropping the football program once seemed to the University of Chicago's Robert Hutchins.

Most of the early, large-scale empirical investigations of the impact ISO 14000 may not have been attentive to the role of such identity factors. Prakash and Potoski's path-breaking study of how the standard affected environmental performance concentrated on firms in the US, where the leaders of most major firms believe that "corporate responsibility is bad capitalism," as the chief executive of Exxon Mobil said in 2003: "We don't invest to make social statements at the expense of shareholder return."[47] In the same year, only 18 percent of the largest companies in the United States provided annual reporting of sustainability issues, in contrast to about 70 percent in Japan and Western Europe.[48]

When ISO 14000 was relatively new, some observers believed that the process that created the standard also meant that it would not be treated as legitimate, or widely adopted, throughout the developing world. In 1998, Jennifer Clapp, now at the Centre for International Governance Innovation in Canada, pointed out that TC-207 Environmental management, "was made up primarily of executives from large multinational firms, standard setting bodies, and consulting firms, while the chairs of the subcommittees and working groups ... all came from industrialized countries, with half the working group chairs being employees of major multinational corporations." In addition, while ISO provided scholarships for 22 developing country delegations, they were much smaller and less effective than those of the industrialized countries.[49] Moreover, in the late 1990s, companies in the developing world could only turn to expensive foreign firms if they wanted to be certified as having met the standard.[50]

Clapp's expectations about the lack of impact of ISO 14000 in the developing world have, to some extent, been met. Consider the pattern of adoptions from 2001 through 2005 (Table 4.1); the bulk of the organizations certified as ISO 14001 compliant remain in Europe. Yet, the ISO 14000 standards *have* become increasingly commonplace in the large and rapidly growing economies of China, Brazil, and India. There is some evidence that "environmental quality" has become one aspect of the identity of at least one part of the private sector in these and other rapidly industrializing counties.

Table 4.1 ISO 14001 certifications by region

	2001		*2005*	
	number	*percent*	*number*	*percent*
Africa and South and West Asia	924	2.5	3,993	3.6
of which India	400		1,698	
East and Southeast Asia	12,796	35.1	46,844	42.1
of which China	1,085		12,683	
Japan	8,123		23,466	
Central and South America	681	1.9	3,411	3.1
of which Brazil	350		2,061	
North America	2,700	7.4	7,119	6.4
Australia/New Zealand	1,422	3.9	2,092	2.3
Europe	17,941	49.2	47,837	43.0

Source: *The ISO Survey—2005* (Geneva, Switzerland: ISO Central Secretariat, 2006), 22–24.

In China, this perhaps surprising environmentalism was promoted by the close relationship between an environmentally committed part of the UN system, the UN Development Programme (UNDP), and many of the most politically influential economic reformers who came to power in the late 1970s.[51] The effort is reflected in the 2008 decision of regulators to require that firms listed on the Beijing Stock Exchange provide a great deal more information about their environmental impact, something that is likely to spur a further explosion of ISO 14000 adoptions.[52]

Even greater commitment is evident in Brazil where, even without a legal requirement, over half of the major national firms publish such reports. Brazil shares some characteristics with other developing countries where reporting on environmental quality and on broader issues of corporate social responsibility has become commonplace.[53] Like China a decade earlier, Brazil in the 1990s made a dramatic shift from an inward-oriented (import-substitution) development strategy to one of openness to the world market and, like China's, Brazil's shift in economic direction was supported by close relations with UN organizations that strongly promoted ecological and social sustainability.[54]

Some Brazilian corporate leaders argue that the country's sponsorship of the UN's 1992 Earth Summit, which took place in Rio de Janeiro, and the 2003 World Social Forum, in Porto Alegre, reflected a general commitment to the proposition that, "a world that is healthy and equitable ... can be built only if sustainability is integrated into the management of corporations, organizations, and the State itself."[55] This commitment certainly reflects the power of environmental and consumer organizations and labor unions; in fact, of a very vibrant civil society that has grown since Brazil's return to electoral democracy in the 1990s, something in keeping with similar patterns in other developing countries where ISO 14000 is widely adopted.[56] In addition, part of Brazil's story is that of other rapidly industrializing countries that have faced major financial crises that originated abroad (e.g. Argentina, Indonesia, and Thailand). A history of such crises has forced Brazilian banks to have close ties to the public sector and to develop an unusually important role in the daily life of many citizens, helping them buffer the wild fluctuations of inflation and devaluation. "Against this backdrop," argue two scholars from Harvard's Hauser Center for Non-Profit Organizations, "banking was one of the first industries in Brazil to consider its role as a corporate citizen."[57] The power of the financial sector, in turn, has influenced firms in other sectors of the Brazilian economy.

Toward a general standard for social responsibility: ISO 26000

The wide interest of Brazilian business leaders in general issues of corporate responsibility, and the similar interest of firms in some other rapidly growing economies, has had a major impact on ISO's current agenda. Since 2003, the organization has been committed to developing a general standard for corporate or "organizational" social responsibility, a standard that would cover environmental sustainability and the promotion of human rights, including the basic rights of workers. In taking on standard setting in this field, ISO is potentially staking out a very large role for itself within global governance. It is also taking on a task at which many other organizations—both public and private— have failed. However, the voluntary consensus process, combined with ISO's experience with management systems and environmental systems standards, may make ISO 26000–Social responsibility a more successful approach to corporate social responsibility than earlier efforts by other NGOs and by the UN.

ISO 26000 responds to a general problem of industrial capitalism: as increasingly productive capitalist firms struggle to find both new markets in which they can sell their goods and the cheapest suppliers, firms push the boundaries of industrial trading areas beyond the regulatory reach of the state, "battering down all Chinese walls."[58] In the nineteenth century, according to Woodrow Wilson, in the days when he was just a political scientist and not yet a promoter of an even more inclusive level of political integration, "society" responded with national integration, pushing up the level of the state—the level of effective regulation—through political integration in Germany, Italy, and the United States.[59]

In the 1930s, with the Great Depression, the push toward larger market areas temporarily ended. Wilson's League of Nations, which was designed both to stop war and to encourage even further economic integration, utterly failed. However, things changed after the Second World War. Powerful governments created free trade organizations, the European Community and the GATT. ISO's work in helping build the infrastructure of a global marketplace was also critically important.

In the 1970s, shortly after container shipping took off, some social movements operating in the developing world began to complain that industrial firms had once again pushed beyond the regulatory reach of the state, citing, for example, Nestlé's strategy for marketing milk formula in Africa. One proposed solution to the general problem was for firms to become subject to binding codes of conduct for a range of issues from marketing and labor practices to relations with host governments, for example, proscribing the payment of kickbacks for government contracts. From the mid-1970s forward, a number of international organizations proposed various codes. They included proposals by a now moribund UN Commission on Transnational Corporations (long opposed by the industrialized countries that provide most of the UN's budget) and the OECD (Organization for Economic Cooperation and Development), the club of rich countries themselves, which proposed a weak code. In addition, in 1977, the International Labor Organization (ILO) passed a frequently updated declaration that lists a set of key ILO conventions and recommendations that should apply to transnational investors.[60]

In the 1990s, in response to growing pressure from consumers and social groups, some firms and social movement organizations established a number of sector-specific standards for corporate responsibility that required third party auditing and provided product labeling. These include Fairtrade (for coffee and other products), Rugmark, the Forestry Stewardship Council, and the Clean Clothes Campaign.[61] In 2000, at the initiative of Secretary General Kofi Annan, the UN began promoting the "Global Compact," under which corporations agreed to support the core ILO labor standards as well as more general human rights standards and the key environmental standards enunciated by various intergovernmental agreements. The Global Compact has no monitoring or enforcement mechanism, although it does require signatory firms to exchange information about best practices and to interact with a group of NGOs that endorse the compact, and act, informally, as its eyes and ears.

University of Manchester political scientist Catia Gregoratti argues that, due to the lack of monitoring, "the Compact ought to be conceptualised not as a neutral institution but as a political elite network which is contributing to the legitimisation of corporate social responsibility and sidelining efforts in support of binding regulation."[62] In part to avoid such criticism, a few corporate leaders almost simultaneously launched a complement—or perhaps an alternative—to the compact called SA (Social Accountability) 8000. SA 8000 is a corporate social responsibility standard that is modeled on ISO 9000 and ISO 14000. Organizations that sign on to the standard must make themselves subject to third party auditing by bodies accredited by the NGO Social Accountability International, which established the standard.[63]

While SA 8000 has a few of the teeth that critics see lacking in the Global Compact, it has none of the legitimacy either of an intergovernmental agreement or of a standard arrived at through the voluntary consensus process. Not surprisingly, then, the debate about establishing a global standard for corporate responsibility continued and ISO was drawn into its center. In May 2001, ISO's consumer committee began researching the possibility of creating such a standard; a year later, this committee's work was taken over by an ad hoc multi-stakeholder investigative committee that reported to the ISO Technical Management Board (TMB) in 2004.[64]

Few members of the investigative committee, which was weighted toward companies and member bodies deeply involved with ISO's management system standards, fundamentally opposed the idea that an ISO process should be set up to arrive at such a general standard for social responsibility. Nevertheless, some committee members were very concerned that the new standard ally itself with those standards that had already been developed by the OECD, ILO, and UN. As a result, ISO sought encouragement from the UN (which it received in 2003) and negotiated "Memoranda of Understanding" with the ILO and the UN agencies supporting the Global Compact.[65] Some NGO representatives on the committee thought it would be financially burdensome to take part in an ISO voluntary consensus process and felt that ISO was a bit undemocratic. Therefore, the investigative committee recommended that ISO allow much broader stakeholder involvement in this process than was typical in the world of a traditional ISO technical committee. Private certification bodies and auditing groups (i.e. those certifiers and auditors that were not also ISO member bodies) were not represented on the investigative committee. In part, this was because some member bodies objected to creating a new, auditable management system standard. Nonetheless, most auditors and certifiers strongly supported the initiative, perhaps anticipating that ISO would eventually agree on a general social responsibility standard that built on its environmental standard just as much as ISO 14000 had built on ISO 9000.[66]

In response to the final report of the advisory committee, the TMB created a fundamentally new kind of "technical committee" to work on the draft standard, to which it gave the number ISO 26000. Two member bodies serve as the secretariat, one from the industrializing "South," Brazil's ABNT (Associação Brasileira de Normas Técnicas), and one from the wealthy "North," Sweden's SIS.[67] The heavy financial burden of the secretariat has been borne by those bodies, by various ministries of the two national governments, and by a number of private firms in both countries that have been involved in the larger movement for corporate social responsibility, including the telecommunications giant Ericsson, Skanska, the global construction firm that is managing the renovation of the UN's New York headquarters, and companies that contribute to Brazil's Ethos Institute, a business NGO supporting social responsibility initiatives.[68]

In choosing the members of the committee, the TMB deliberately de-emphasized the traditional norm of focusing on the companies who will finance and use the standard; instead, they have placed much greater emphasis on the other ISO norms of having the widest possible representation and of assuring that "experts" in the field are very active in any discussions.[69] The result is a working group of about 400 people, which the joint secretariat has also tried to balance in terms of gender, ethnicity, and primary interest within "social responsibility," (e.g. labor, indigenous rights, conservation, etc.). It is also the first time that much of an ISO committee's work has been completely open. The secretariat made the committee's electronic communication public, and, in response to public protests by consumer groups at the May 2006 plenary meeting, planned to make the face-to-face meetings more open, as well.[70]

At its first meetings, the negotiating committee quickly agreed that ISO 26000 would create a standard covering seven fields: (1) corporate governance and transparency, (2) the environment, (3) human rights, (4) labor practices, (5) fair operating practices, (6) consumer issues, and (7) community development and involvement. In many of the fields, existing UN standards and, of course, ISO 14000, provided ready guidelines.[71]

In January 2008, the Swedish head of the joint secretariat, Kristina Sandberg, who also leads the QMS and EMS division of SIS, was hesitant to predict that the ISO 26000 negotiations would be successful, but she was convinced that because so many stakeholders were contributing to the process, any result would be "strongly anchored in a global desire to make the standard work."[72] Kristina Tamm Hallström, a scholar of standardization known for her pointed criticism of ISO processes, makes a similar point about the committee negotiating ISO 26000, "[I]t appears that ISO succeeded in creating a legitimate organization [the negotiating committee] by taking the time to creatively respond to points made by its critics."[73]

However, the process of creating an *effective* social responsibility standard is far from over. The current process, which is expected to result in a consensus standard by 2010, does not address the issues of auditing and certification—things that would help provide the "teeth" to the ISO standard that some of its competitors, like the Global Compact, do not have. Sandberg admits that such teeth "may develop at a later date," and her own background as SIS's point person for management systems suggests that the secretariat is expecting that to happen, but firms that want to avoid any real monitoring of (say) their labor practices or their impact on local communities are going to object.

Nonetheless, John Ruggie, the political scientist who worked with Kofi Annan to design the Global Compact and who serves as the UN secretary general's special representative for business and human rights, argues that we are likely to see increasing demands for globally recognized standards of good corporate behavior *from corporations* if only because of "the growing potential for companies to be held liable for international crimes" by the International Criminal Court, various ad hoc international tribunals, and the regional international courts whose jurisdictions now cover almost every part of the world.[74] Certification of adherence to a comprehensive ISO 26000 could come to serve as proof of innocence to these courts in the same way that national enforcement of ISO technical standards serves as proof of innocence under the GATT/WTO Standards Code. Moreover, the WTO Standards Code itself may encourage firms to adopt ISO 26000, just as it has encouraged adoption of the management systems standards that preceded it.

However, enforcement of a unified global code of corporate social responsibility may not be a panacea for all the problems of a weakly regulated global economy. A group of South African social scientists acknowledges that if a global social responsibility standard included an auditing mechanism, it would allow the South African government to husband its regulatory resources and focus on firms that are non-compliant. On the other hand, it is unlikely, they argue, that any global standard will highlight the corporate activities that are socially the most important in any particular context. For example, in South Africa, the government-mandated Black Economic Empowerment initiative is concerned with increasing the black share of the private sector and management positions in all sectors, goals that are unlikely to be at the center of any global standard.[75]

There is a more general problem involved with establishing a global standard for corporate responsibility: in many fields, the interests of the majority in the global "North" and the majority within the global "South" differ. For example, consider labor conditions. Industrial workers in the North tend to favor the highest possible standards, and are often willing to sacrifice the benefits of free trade to put pressure on non-conforming companies in the South. On the other hand, unions in the South are much more likely to be interested in the jobs that free trade creates; they often see Northern champions of "higher global labor standards" as self-interested protectionists.[76] Peter Utting of the UN Research Institute for Social Development argues, more generally, that in most global corporate social responsibility discussions, "priority issues are often those of particular concern to activists and others in the North. ... Interests relevant to particular stakeholders in developing countries, such as women workers, sometimes get short shrift." The problem is compounded by the fact that all existing standards, "curb specific types of malpractice and improve selected aspects of social performance without questioning various contradictory policies and practices that can have perverse consequences in terms of equality and equity."[77] Michael J. Watts, who studies oil companies in the developing world, writes about firms that live up to "social responsibility" pledges to investment in the local economy by hiring local mercenaries to enforce the companies' exploitative policies.[78]

Watts's experience convinces him that the only valuable social responsibility standards would be those that are constantly monitored and backed by strong incentives to comply. If an actual standard emerges from the ISO negotiations, its eventual effectiveness or lack of effectiveness will undoubtedly be linked to rapid establishment of a monitoring system and to the presence of "enforcers"—individuals and firms that will only buy ISO 26000 compliant goods and services, national regulators who use information about compliance with the standard to identify violators of legally mandated standards, and the possible pressure that might come from international criminal courts and the WTO Standards Code.

In addition, questions of organizational identity may come to play a role in the spread of ISO 26000 just as they did with ISO 9000 and ISO 14000. Some of the power of organizations identifying themselves with "social responsibility" has already been visible in the negotiations over the standard. Tamm Hallström characterizes the work of the negotiating committee as a process of learning to overcome many of the North–South conflicts of interest that have stymied other attempts to negotiate effective corporate codes of conduct since the 1970s. In addition, if Kristina Sandberg's (perhaps self-interested) assessment is correct, the ISO process itself is leading to a widespread desire "to make the standard work" as well as to an expectation that many organizations will adopt the standard immediately simply because they have been involved in the process and have become invested in it or because they model themselves on other organizations that have been deeply involved in the process.[79]

If ISO 26000 proves successful, then the longer story that connects that standard back to ISO's work on quality and environmental standards will provide strong evidence that engagement in voluntary consensus standard setting leads participants to a more "civic" view of the role of corporations. In early 2008, Nalle Sturén, the widow of ISO's longest-serving secretary general, mused, "Either only nice people work with standardization, or working with standardization makes you nice."[80] The analysis of voluntary consensus standard setting that has long convinced some observers that this engineering process could be used to design effective, progressive social regulation would expect Sturén's second hypothesis be the one that explains what she has observed over more than 50 years.

Conclusion

ISO, today, seems to be fulfilling, at least partially, the social promise of voluntary consensus standard setting that was anticipated over a century ago. ISO's early work on quality management—an agenda that came to the organization in a roundabout way, championed by some governments concerned with the competitiveness of their firms in increasingly global markets—proved remarkably successful. ISO built on its QMS by creating a widely adopted Environmental Management System, ISO 14000, and a host of additional environmental standards that have helped control of pollution. Many of the same actors who supported ISO's move into the environmental field, have also championed its current attempt to set a general standard for corporate social responsibility that would cover labor and human rights issues as well. When ISO entered the field, there were already other important CSR initiatives, partially based on voluntary consensus standard setting principles. At the time of writing (in 2008), we are witnessing an important real-world experiment. If those who have long anticipated the social promise of voluntary consensus standard setting are correct, ISO's venture into the CSR field should prove more successful than its contemporary alternatives, such as the UN Global Compact, because ISO more fully embraces all aspects of the voluntary consensus model.

5 Standards wars and the future of ISO

Even though voluntary consensus standard setting now plays a growing role in global governance in domains far from its original technical fields, many observers see ISO becoming less and less relevant to standard setting in its original milieu: the leading sectors and most technologically advanced industries throughout the world. Since the 1980s, when the Commission of the European Union began an aggressive program aimed at rapidly producing new industrial standards relevant to Europe, its major trading partner, the United States, has accused Europe of hijacking the ISO process and attempting to establish EU standards as global standards. At the same time, many firms and high-tech engineers in those fields have abandoned the voluntary consensus process in favor of one of two alternatives, proprietary standards formed by cooperating companies, "consortia," and open source processes in which many high-technology engineers—some of them honored veterans of recent standards wars—are working to make those conflicts "but a prelude to the main act, which is now opening—the free sharing of information, and eventually, one hopes, knowledge."[1] That is a drama in which ISO may only have a small role to play.

The conflict between Europe and the United States

After the United States' most famous standards' champion, Herbert Hoover, failed to halt the Great Depression, social scientists' interest in voluntary consensus standard setting waned, especially in the United States. The recent widespread revival of research has had different sources in different fields. In political science and sociology, the US–European conflict over standardization in high-technology fields has been one source of the new interest.

In a widely cited 2003 article in *World Politics*, Walter Mattli and Tim Büthe depict standard setting as a game among the great powers.[2]

If a great power can establish its own national product standards as global standards it gives significant first mover advantages to its firms. The EU, the argument goes, is able to establish new standards faster than the United States because the European standard setting system has an element of central direction that is not found in the United States. Moreover, European firms have much closer and more formal links to their governments than do firms in the United States; thus, European firms can more easily make their preferences into government preferences. Supporting these European advantages, other analysts argue, is the fact that the EU's internal market is now larger than that of the United States, which gives manufactures in every part of the world a greater incentive to conform to European standards than to US standards.[3]

There are many reasons for the interest in these hypotheses. They resonate with the tough-minded "power and purpose" theories that dominate the study of international relations in the US—the "neorealist" theories that emphasize the power and purpose of states and the "neoliberal" theories that link international behavior to economic models of the profit-maximizing firm. These closely related "neo-neo" theories[4] present a sharp challenge to those of one prominent group of sociologists, the "world-polity school," who see the history of voluntary consensus standard setting as the unfolding of a global culture of rationality, individualism, progress, and universalism.[5] Similarly, a paradigmatic 1991 study by one of the most prominent US "realists," Stephen D. Krasner, explains the government-controlled process of standard setting in the International Telecommunication Union (ITU) as a consequence of national interests and power and *not* a manifestation of the engineering rationality that ITU claimed to share with ISO.[6] Standing somewhat between the world-polity sociologists and the neo-neos in political science is the relatively new field of economic sociology. The stylized fact of a consequential difference between a more statist European system of standard setting and a more market-based approach in the United States resonates with the main justification for the new field, the argument that the sociologists' insights into organizational structures are crucial to understanding economic outcomes in the real world.[7]

It is possible to critique some the arguments made in the 2003 Mattli and Büthe article. For instance, the authors seem to date the "largely anarchic US system" from 1960 when the American National Standards Institute (ANSI) adopted its current name. In fact, the US national body was one of the first to be established and has been at the center of the global movement for standardization from near the beginning.

Similarly, the authors point to the scores of member organizations that make up ANSI and ignore the similar structure of the other leading national bodies, including those that are formally part of their national government.[8] Moreover, the article's conclusion that, "the organizational characteristics of the European standardization system make for a more felicitous match between the national and international institutions than the characteristics of the largely anarchic American system,"[9] is suspiciously similar to claims made by ANSI (on the part of a few of its members) that pan-European standardizing activity was inherently unfair, claims that the American standards guru Carl F. Cargill and IT strategy consultant Sherrie Bolin dismiss as "shrill" and "not helpful to the [US] IT (information technology) industry."[10]

Still, there certainly are some classic, consequential cases of European firms gaining international markets through government-facilitated technical standards. Consider GSM (Global System for Mobile) the most widely used mobile telephone standard. It was created by a group of engineers at a French national laboratory in 1982 and adopted in 1987 by an agreement among most of the EU telephone providers (when most of them were still government agencies, before the widespread privatization of the 1990s).[11] Due to the global significance of the EU market, the standard was rapidly adopted in the rest of Europe, Africa, and much of Asia and Latin America and this did hurt some US companies. Back in early 2004, when we wanted to have mobile phones that would connect us both in Boston, Massachusetts and in much of the world our only real choice was to sign up with a company called T-Mobile, otherwise known as Deutsche Telekom, the former state-owned monopoly (privatized in 1996) that had helped establish GSM.

Princeton economist Paul Krugman draws a different lesson from this "classic case" than the one drawn by some US firms; he sees it as just a consequence of the ideological thrall of free-market economics on the western side of the Atlantic:

I have a T-Mobile cell phone, which uses GSM technology; it works all over the world—and in parts of New Jersey. One of the parts of New Jersey in which it doesn't work happens to be my own home. As a result, I have been acutely aware of the price America paid for not doing what Europe did and settling on a single mobile standard. ... [D]efenders of the American non-system ... [talked of] spurring competition that would lead to faster technological progress. Never mind. ... Europe has stayed ahead of the US ... Having one technology standard has spurred competition among network operators and handset manufacturers while competition in the US has been stymied by a proliferation of standards.[12]

However, the issue may not just be one of American ideological pigheadedness. Historical institutionalists point out that, in Herbert Hoover's day, conservative leaders on both sides of the Atlantic were trying to build productive institutional arrangements that would both allow private business groups direct access into industrial policy making and preserve productive economic competition. Hoover called his vision of the desired outcome "the Associational State"; today, political scientists refer to it as "corporatism." Unfortunately for Hoover and likeminded leaders, the structure of the US party system meant that many of the American business associations became captives of the one party of the right, sort of lobbying groups for the Republicans. In contrast, in Sweden (for example), business people could express their political convictions through a number of political parties, including Christian Democrats, Moderates, and the Folkpartiet, under whose banner Olle Sturén once served as mayor of his Stockholm suburb. In multi-party democracies, the early twentieth-century "corporatist" structures created to bring business groups (and labor unions) directly into national economic planning did not degenerate into forums for partisan posturing, which was what tended to happen in the United States.[13]

Yet, both US businesses and scholars who focus on the difference between US and European institutions may overestimate the degree to which Europe's corporatist structures have been able to create powerful "European standards." Recall from Chapter 1 how local standard setters have often been able to thwart the desire of central governments to impose uniform standards at a larger scale. Many European standard setters see this problem repeated in the EU, and are surprised at US ignorance of this pattern.[14]

Other Europeans see their recurrent standards wars with the United States as a consequence of the strategies typically adopted by US businesses when they operate outside their home market. Olle Sturén believed that there was a range of typical national business strategies and that they had shaped the major conflicts within ISO. Japanese firms—motivated, in part, by the customer orientation of the quality management ideology—were typically geared to produce different products in different markets, and therefore Japan originally took something of a lackadaisical attitude toward the development of global standards. US firms, at the other extreme, typically attempted to sell abroad exactly the same products that they had developed for their own, huge national market, so American businesses typically had a keen interest in making "American standards" "international standards," hence the periodic US impulse to do battle with Europe over standards.[15]

Sturén was certainly right about the recurrent pattern, but he did not emphasize the degree to which each round of the US–European conflict was initiated by a (typically, unsuccessful) attempt by the European Commission (the executive branch of the EU) to promote Europe-wide standards.

Hans Micklitz, who holds the Jean Monnet Chair of Private Law and European Economic Law at the University of Bamberg, blandly notes that the first attempt by the European Commission, in the 1960s, "proved to be a failure."[16] French standard setter Jean-Pierre Galland points out that the commission allowed individual member states to impose their own health and safety standards on products and services while insisting that other industrial standards be Community-wide. Most members used some of those "legal" standards to protect national industries.[17] Historian Marine Moguen-Toursel considers the issue through the lens of the history of the automobile industry. One of the aims of the commission, in the 1960s and 1970s, was to promote European automobile firms that could successfully compete with Japanese firms, at least within the European market, without resorting to protectionist measures. However, the national exceptions allowed to European standards, and the overall complexity of intergovernmental agreements that were negotiated, ended up maintaining essentially national markets for motor vehicles for another generation.[18]

Yet, despite the failure of the commission's first round attempt to legislate Europe-wide standards in order to promote European industry, many US firms worried that they would end up being excluded from the EU market by the imposition of such standards. Therefore, US companies lobbied their government to push for the GATT (General Agreement on Tariffs and Trade) Standards Code, which, ironically, increased the global impact of voluntary consensus standard setting and strengthened ISO.[19]

A second major attempt by the commission had a similar outcome. In the mid-1980s, it began working to change its standards policy with the "aim to strengthen European industry."[20] The European Community's executive branch commissioned a number of policy papers and began negotiations with Europe's non-governmental voluntary consensus standard setting body, CEN (the European Committee for Standardization), with its affiliate concerned with electrotechnical issues, and with ISO and the IEC (International Electrotechnical Commission). In those negotiations, the non-governmental bodies pointed to the principles embodied in the GATT (now WTO, World Trade Organization) Standards Code and to the fundamental norm underlying voluntary consensus standard setting since its beginning: the point of standard setting is to encourage productive competition, not to restrict trade. Moreover, ISO argued, governments often fail when they try to set standards.

Tineke Egyedi, senior researcher on IT standardization at the Delft University of Technology, demonstrates that ISO's arguments largely won the day. In a 1992 Green Paper (a first draft of its new policy), "the Commission cedes to most of ISO/IEC's criticisms. It concedes that international standards should be the primary aim of European standardization." Yet, even though the Commission accepts ISO arguments, it "still pursues a Eurocentric standards policy." The Green Paper tells ISO that its standard setting must be done in a timely manner; if an important standard is not produced quickly by the voluntary consensus mechanism, the EU will reserve the right to legislate an alternative. Moreover, the EU will only accept new product standards that take certain "European requirements," primarily about health and safety, into account.[21] In a sense, the Commission simply reaffirmed its own role in the kind of system that the classic article by economists Joseph Farrell and Garth Saloner demonstrated as the most effective: standard setting by technical committees operating under consensus rules in a world in which powerful actors (dominant firms, leading states, or a formally organized trading region such as the EU) can defect from the process and set a standard that many others are likely to follow.[22]

The current round of the US–EU standards war has a lot to do with two facts: (1) that in some fields many others (companies in Asia, Africa, and Latin America, and even many companies in the United States) are likely to follow an EU standard if the EU defects from the ISO process, and (2) it is probably harder for ANSI or the US Congress to develop alternative "American standards" around which others might rally.

Yet, many of these worries may be largely *theoretical*, the concerns of a very small number of companies that ANSI feels it must represent with that "shrill" rhetoric that frustrates some American standard setters like Cargill. After all, as Cargill and Bolin put it, carrying out the battle with Europe puts many US companies—and perhaps the entire IT industry—in something of a dilemma. Either IT companies have to disown ANSI, which is the only organization empowered to represent

US interests in the ISO system, or else those companies have to act as if they accept the nonsense that ANSI and the US government embrace when confronting the EU, "the concept of an overriding US national position" on all standards issues.[23] In fact, most of the *actual* issues that bother US companies about European standards should have very little implication for ISO, and some could even be considered as major utilitarian benefits of the global voluntary consensus standard setting system.

At an open forum held by the Department of Commerce in early 2005, US companies complained about three kinds of issues.[24] First was the fact that American firms face a multitude of different standards regimes across Europe—a complaint that the EU Commission shares. Second, are a set of problems connected with one of the principles governing European safety and health "requirements," the so-called "precautionary principle" in dealing with new technologies. This principle, which holds in the absence of a scientific consensus that harm would not ensue from employing a new technology, that the burden of proof falls on those who advocate doing so, has led the EU to impose a rigorous system of mandatory testing of all new chemicals (similar to the US system of testing drugs for human use) and bans on the use of most genetically modified organisms (GMOs) in agriculture. Finally, some US companies worried about the developing world adopting "non-market driven" standards such as ISO 14000, the environmental management standard that is much more commonly adhered to in Europe than in the United States.

The second of these sets of concerns focuses on regulations by European governments, not on the voluntary consensus realm of ISO, while, arguably, both these "precautionary principle" concerns and worries that the EU is "exporting its [sic] standards" (e.g. ISO 14000) to developing countries may, in fact, be beneficial to most citizens of the United States. As one participant at the Commerce Department forum put it, "Consumers want the US and EU to focus on best practices and to 'harmonize up.'"[25] In the early 1980s, when today's neorealist and neoliberal "power and purpose" theories were brand new, one of the questions that animated the US scholars who developed those theories was, "In the future, who will provide the global public goods?" that those scholars believed the United States had provided immediately after the Second World War—things like the Marshall Plan and monetary stability maintained by gold–dollar convertibility—now that the United States no longer had the "hegemonic power" to do so or the related "purpose" to maintain its dominance in a benign way.[26] Arguably, the ISO system, backed by the conditions under which the EU will defect from it, has created an alternative provider of significant "global public goods." ISO 14000 and 26000 may some day come to be seen in the United States as Europe's payback for the Marshall Plan to a country whose peculiar political institutions make it difficult for it to set progressive standards by itself.

Even so, there are certainly ways in which the EU's preferences about standards are not necessarily in the interest of the entire world. In a recent book, *Starved for Science: How Biotechnology is Being Kept Out of Africa*, political scientist Robert Paarlberg argues that while the EU precautionary-principle-based opposition to GMO food may do no harm to Europeans, or to people who have enjoyed the benefits of the non-GMO-based green revolutions in Asia and Latin America, European pressure on African governments to adopt the same standards may be preventing a similar revolution in the continent where the most people are hungry.[27] If, as many European standard setting bodies insist, the precautionary principle is incorporated into ISO 26000, some observers will certainly come to see the global organization as complicit in an African tragedy.

Moreover, even if it is largely the interests of only a few US companies that are fueling the current US–EU standards war, the dissatisfaction of those companies, and the strategic actions of the EU Commission, call into question some of the rosier assessments of voluntary consensus standard setting as a means of overcoming particular interests. Moreover, Jean-Pierre Galland points out that even the somewhat modest increase in influence that the EU Commission has gained over global standard setting since the 1980s has come at the cost of excluding not only the voices of some US companies, but also the voices of many interest groups within Europe—smaller businesses operating in very local markets, most labor organizations, and much of civil society. Galland, a believer in the usual arguments in favor of voluntary consensus standard setting, believes that if this trend of exclusion were to continue, the result, ultimately, would be a disaster—a system of standards and regulation with very little legitimacy. However, he points to the conviction of prominent European standard setters that this era of exclusion is coming to an end and that by (say) 2015 many more parties will involved in most European, and ISO, standard setting.[28]

Greater inclusiveness may help end this round of the standards war between Europe and the United States, but it may make other problems that currently threaten ISO even more difficult to solve. Usually when there are more parties to negotiations, it takes longer to reach agreement. However, right now, there is significant pressure on ISO to reach agreements ever more quickly.

Wars over IT standards

That pressure comes from the rapidity of technological change in the fields of communication and information processing. Often, although perhaps misleadingly, analysts point to the source of that change by citing "Moore's Law," first articulated by Fairchild Semiconductor's Gordon Moore in 1965 and often summarized as, "computing power at fixed cost doubles every 18 months."[29] Rapidly increasing computing power leads to the almost exponential proliferation of new devices that employ or link computers and of the software that makes them work. To turn all that computing power into coherent, beneficial—or, at least, highly profitable—systems requires the equally rapid development of thousands of new standards.

In 1987, ISO responded to the IT explosion by adopting "fast track" procedures that allow a proposed standard to be published as soon as it is widely accepted within a technical committee.[30] In 1990, ISO and IEC officials began to argue that their processes could be sped up even further by excluding many of the parties that had traditionally been represented, even user industries. After all, *"an emerging technology has no users* ... As such, negotiations for these agreements do not need to be conducted under the traditional multi-interest consensus procedures."[31]

Despite these changes, ISO lost control of the IT standard setting process. In the 1990s, "dozens of standards committees, industry consortia, and *ad hoc* alliances strove to exercise authority over standards for new digital networks."[32] All of these potential standard setters faced the opposition of two powerful forces: the anarchistic culture embraced by many software engineers and the hope of many companies that one of their own key technologies would become a de facto standard, thus allowing the company to reap monopoly profits.

A concise summary of the norms shared by many engineers can be found in the unofficial motto of the Internet Engineering Task Force (IETF), the open club of engineers that "has no legal status and no defined membership, yet has played a central role in governing the Internet since its beginning."[33] In 1992, David Clark, a leading Internet architect, declared, "We reject: kings, presidents, and voting. We believe in: rough consensus and running code."[34] According to telecommunications historian Andrew L. Russell,

> This phrase ... encapsulated the IETF's rejection of hierarchical decision-making ... and preference instead for iterative networking experiments that garner a widespread consensus. The ... commitment

to "running code" represents a jab at the competing set of standards for internetworking created by ... ISO [whose] process lacked experimental value and flexibility while at the same time suffering from excessive bureaucratic constraints.[35]

Software engineers "adopted 'pure-play' strategies in order to focus closely on complex and narrowly defined engineering problems,"[36] but such strategies encouraged the creation of divergent, and potentially incompatible, products, such as the many "dialects" of key computer languages that tend to develop in different research laboratories.[37]

At the other extreme, many IT companies refused to engage in negotiations about significant standards in the hope that their own proprietary standard would become the global norm. After all, this had been the business strategy of the most successful of the IT companies, Microsoft, whose proprietary Windows software governs the basic operation of most personal computers throughout the world. In popular parlance, the phrase "standards wars" now most often refers to these "winner-take-all situations" in which a few big companies vie for monopoly control over some digital gateway technology—for example, the recent conflict between Blu-ray and HD DVD standards for the new generation of video recordings.[38]

For ISO, the problem of companies profiting from proprietary control of any component of a standard is particularly difficult. The ISO norm is that its standards can be completely implemented—without paying rents or royalties—by anyone who has the 50 or 100 Swiss francs to buy a copy of the document. Indeed, the ISO commitment to having its standards represent a kind of open and unencumbered transfer of technology has, if anything, grown in recent decades. Moreover, this ISO (and IEC) norm has been increasingly adopted by the intergovernmental International Telecommunication Union (ITU), which also plays a major role in IT standardization.[39] Yet, in the IT field, many users are willing to accept, and even desire, some standards that include some proprietary components—especially software components that "the market" has made a de facto standard. Yet, despite all these difficulties, ISO and IEC's joint committee on information technology (JTC-1) is the most active of ISO's technical committees. It produces far more standards than any other committee does. How can that be?

Well, for one thing, there is some evidence that participation by IT companies in standard setting committees, perhaps even in unsuccessful committees, facilitates future alliances by innovative firms.[40] "This effect is magnified by sustained participation by individuals on behalf of firms," so there is a reason to be there for the long haul. Such meetings are especially important in bringing the less established (and, in the IT field, perhaps often the most innovative) firms into alliance networks. Established firms have a clear incentive to take part in technical committees, to find sources of new talent and new products. So do less established firms, to find established business partners who can help them grow.

Cargill and Bolin explain, less speculatively, that the formal standard setting arena remains extremely important to the IT field as a whole because it provides stable, non-experimental standards that are essential to some applications.[41] For example, in many IT applications, information security is indispensable. Consider bank-to-bank transfers of funds, on-line purchasing, and "groupware" software that allows product developers in different sites to work on the same innovation. Not surprisingly, perhaps, JTC-1, the intergovernmental ITU, and even the anarchistic IETF have become an effective, interdependent mechanism for setting standards designed to solve "an ever increasing set of security issues."[42]

One of the main secrets to this successful collaboration is the fact that the individual participants in all of these standard setting forums are essentially the same. IETF may have no legal status or defined membership and it may call its operating principles "The Tao," its meetings "gatherings of the tribe,"[43] and its published standards "Requests for Comment,"[44] but most of IETF's "non-members" are just as comfortable working in the more structured virtual space, or the more formal physical meetings, of JCT-1. For example, IBM's vice president for "Open Source and Standards," Bob Sutor, calls himself an "evangelist" for "open source" (the principle that software should be freely redistributed) and his web site is full of "software geek" references. The most prominent link is to the "Make Poverty History" initiative and much of the site seems to be about Bob Dylan, Bruce Springsteen, and various science fiction series. Yet, Sutor is pictured in the traditional IBM grey flannel suit and his daily blog is more about discussions in JCT-1 than it is about Dr. Who.[45]

In fact, even the most evangelically free-spirited software engineer is apt to have something of a love–hate relationship with ISO. Much of the innovative work in the IT industry over the last two decades has been framed within a particular conceptual model of potential system components (hardware as well as software) and the possible ways in which all such components could interconnect, seamlessly. That model, OSI (the Open Systems Interconnection architecture), adopted in 1984, was perhaps the last major innovation of ISO during the Olle Sturén era.[46] It conceptualizes the links between computers or groups of computers as operating at seven layers from the "Physical" (mechanical and electrical characteristics such as connector sizes, pin assignments, and voltage levels) to the "Application" layer, which includes features that allow multiple users of the same program to share information (Figure 5.1).

OSI has been an essential enabler of systems development—a way to conceptualize and discuss new components and their place in larger, interconnected computer systems. At the same time, the model generated an incredible amount of wasted standard-setting effort within JTC-1, the creation of scores of "anticipatory standards," efforts to standardize new information technologies in advance of a "specific technology being available in any viable commercial form." Cargill writes, "[T]he standardization effort expanded to cover nearly every possible contingency. ... Because of the number of options available, an OSI system provider could both comply to the OSI standards and be totally inoperable with other systems."[47]

This development, which was apparent by the early 1990s, led companies to form more limited "consortia" to create standards that actually worked in the real world—standards that could provide a guarantee to consumers that certain products really would work together. However, the consortia were often designed to promote the use of one company's proprietary technology; they assured that a range of products truly would work well together, at least for users who had

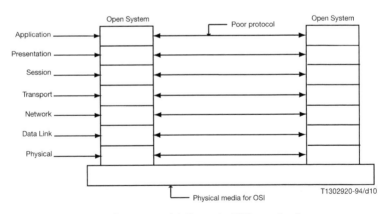

Figure 5.1 The OSI reference model (from the ISO standard).
Source: ISO/IEC International Standard 7498-1, Information Technology–Open Systems–Interconnection–Basic Reference Model: The Basic Model, 2nd ed., 15 November 1994, Corrected and reprinted 15 June 1996, 34.

purchased a particular gateway technology, for example, an operating system like Microsoft Windows. That was repugnant to many open-source-oriented engineers.[48]

Moreover, as Andrew Russell points out, it was open-source-oriented engineers in IETF who developed and maintained the data exchange protocols that the Internet actually uses. The process of developing ISO standards for each of the seven layers just proved too bureaucratic and slow. Russell quotes one engineer involved in both ISO and IETF standardization as noting the irony that, in the early 1990s, "There we were solemnly anointing international standards for networking, and every time we needed to send electronic mail or exchange files, we were using ... TCP/IP," the alternative protocol development by IETF.[49]

Nevertheless, Cargill and Bolin see ISO and even those industry consortia that are hated by open-source-oriented engineers as necessary, even if some consortia are just a necessary evil. ISO provides the greatest stability. Consortia fulfill "the need for defined and structured faster change."[50] They usually deal with relatively restricted problems to overcome concrete incompatibilities and most consortia are relatively short-lived. Cargill cites the Unicode Consortium, active throughout the 1990s, as one of the best. In the 1980s, ISO had set a standard for digitally representing character sets from different languages, but the organization was slow to add sets for additional languages or to deal with glitches as they came up, so major companies—including Microsoft, Xerox, and Apple—established a consortium to take up the slack. After a few years, technology moved on and, in Cargill's view, the need for a separate standard setter in this field disappeared, but, at a critical point, the Unicode Consortium had done its work well.[51]

Most of the existing consortia have been exclusively oriented toward the US market. Large European firms are never essential partners. In part, this is because a major role that the consortia have played is the promotion of standard gateway technologies like Windows. Major European firms interested in promoting similar gateway technologies—e.g. GSM—can rely on voluntary consensus standard setting bodies, backed up by the credible threat of official standard setting if the voluntary process proves too slow. In the more market-oriented United States, firms typically must use market power—developed and secured by special alliances with other companies—to achieve the same end.[52]

Yet, not all alliance-seeking American IT firms have business strategies aimed at controlling a technology that somehow becomes essential to almost all computer users. At the center of Sun Microsystems' strategy, for example, is the company's freely downloadable Web applications language, Java. Sun has, however, been very concerned with standardizing, updating, and maintaining the integrity of Java. At one point, the company even asked ISO to carry out that role, but eventually withdrew its support for ISO, fearing that Java would get out of Sun's control and that ISO might manage the language in a way that benefited the company's competitors.[53]

Like other companies in similar situations, Sun turned from ISO to an ad hoc consortium of allied companies that maintains Java. However, due to the suspicion that many open source advocates have of such consortia—the suspicion that they exist only to promote the narrow economic interests of the sponsoring firm—private companies that try to maintain the integrity of open source technologies are constantly tempted to avoid consortia and go back to the publicly oriented standard setters, like ISO.[54]

An alternative way to achieve the legitimacy—and wide use—of a free software product that is meant to be a gateway technology is to forget standardization by technical committees and completely embrace the non-commercial norms of the "open source movement" that came to unify many open-source-oriented engineers by the beginning of this century.[55] Berkeley political scientist Steven Weber, argues that, at its most expansive, the movement aims to shift the central concern of modern industrial economies from profit making to knowledge sharing, but, in more immediate terms, the movement unites a community whose shared purpose is to compete with proprietary approaches to information technology, like that of Microsoft.[56]

There have certainly been successful products—and even successful companies—that have been rooted in the open source movement. The operating system, Linux, which is the most widely used competitor to Microsoft's main product, as well as Sun Microsystems's Java, are cases in point. Andrew Russell argues that among the developers of Linux and many of its applications, "Tensions between rule creation and rule enforcement have largely been kept at bay through a grassroots culture that stresses openness, sharing, and compatibility more than commercial gain."[57] Cargill and Bolin make the more general argument that when an organization developing or promoting a open source product feels the need for legitimacy and expertise that can only come from "complete community involvement," then it must look to solve the standardization problem by completely embracing open source norms.[58]

Tineke Egyedi and Ruben van Wendel de Joode point out that, at least on the surface, the seemingly "anything goes" norms of the open source movement seem to be opposed to those of traditional standard setters. Yet, in fact, a number of processes adopted by the open source community end up serving the same function of stabilizing a technology that is the one performed by an effective standard. In particular, Egyedi and van Wendel de Joode point to the coordinating role of "bandwagoning": if an open source technology—such as the Linux operating system—is extremely successful, each new user has strong incentives both to maintain the core of the technology (the elements that assure that it can be used across a large network of users) and to encourage others to use the technology.[59]

Moreover, many open source technologies, including the Internet protocols, have been developed within large committees of engineers that operate very much like technical committees do when a new technology is needed to establish a broader standard (for example, when tests proved that a new kind of container corner was needed, see page 58). The only major difference is that open source committees, such as of IETF, have few restrictions on their membership other than the non-formalized norm that anyone who takes part has to be expert enough to understand what is going on.[60]

However, at this point, it is not at all clear how the open source movement will develop, whether it will transcend the current social need for more formal mechanisms for technological standardization, let alone the need to profit from new knowledge. Many of its leading figures seem to exist in two worlds, as Bob Sutor's job title at IBM suggests: "Vice President for Open Source and Standards." Yet, for the foreseeable future, it is seems clear that both ISO and a changing array of consortia will continue to have roles to play in the rapidly moving high-technology fields. A recent, cleverly designed study by Timothy S. Simcoe and Marc Rysman uses a massive sample of US high-technology patent citations to assess whether the voluntary consensus standard setting bodies remain influential, especially as compared to a group of firm-centered consortia as well as the open-source-oriented IETF. It is clear that the voluntary consensus standards still matter. The patent record shows that the standards created by ISO and related organizations both "identify" and "select" key technologies—technologies that will affect future technological development—as significantly as standards created by IETF and the consortia.[61]

Conclusion

In sum, ISO's immediate future is far from simple. In the highest-technology fields, the kinds of fields that were the source of the international standards movement more than a century ago, ISO is likely to continue to share the job of standard setting with consortia supporting proprietary technologies and with the open source movement. In older technological fields (except those dealt with by the intergovernmental World Health Organization), and in the field of quality management, ISO is likely to remain at the center of standard setting throughout the world. This is a consequence of the fact that, in the globally connected economy that has existed since the late 1980s, the focus of most national standard setting bodies has been on creating international standards. Despite the periodic outbursts of suspicion that some major states, and especially the EU, have tried to gain economic advantage through domination of the ISO process, there is little reason to believe that the recent international standards wars will reduce ISO's role in the world economy, or that of the voluntary consensus standard setting network as a whole.

6   Conclusion

The International Organization for Standardization, ISO, has existed
for over 60 years. It has helped set industrial standards that touch
almost every aspect of human life. Even if we retreat as far away from
the world of industrial products as we possibly can, ISO standards will
follow us. If we escape to an untouched wilderness—to a mountain
park or to an island beach—there will still be ISO standards that define
some parts of the backpack we carry with us, the water bottle that hangs
from it, and even the water that bottle contains. Our hiking boots or
our swimming suits probably came from the factories where they were
made to stores where we bought them in ISO standard containers and
the train, bus, boat, or car that took us to our pre-industrial idyll
contained hundreds of ISO standard parts, many of them made under
the eye of an ISO standard quality management system.

Yet, for all of the ubiquity of ISO's standards, few people ever think
about them, or about the process by which they are created and
adopted. Nevertheless, for as long as this process has existed, there
have always been a few political thinkers who have believed that that
process was particularly important. ISO standards are adopted voluntarily, and they are created by the consensus of representatives of those
who will use and those who will produce the products and services to
which they apply. Ever since engineers invented voluntary consensus
standard setting, there have men who have imagined that the process
could be used to reach agreement on a whole range of progressive
regulation that governments (for one reason or another) fail to provide.

Voluntary consensus standard setting predates ISO by almost as
many years as ISO has existed, but, from the beginning, many of the
believers in the importance of the process were convinced that such
standard setting ultimately had to be done at a global level. After all,
standards helped define the limits of economic units, of trading areas,
and the industrial system would provide its greatest benefits (the standard

setters believed) if a single, global economic unit could be formed. The goal, from the beginning, was international standards.

Nonetheless, throughout most of the twentieth century, and even in the first two decades after ISO was created, most standard setting work operated at the level of the nation-state. The most important organizations were national standard setting bodies and it was national standard setting bodies—many of them private associations made up, themselves, of other private associations—that established ISO.

By the 1980s, though, most of the work of the national standard setting bodies, groups like BSI (the British Standards Institution, the oldest of the national bodies and the model for many of them) focused on setting global standards. Much of this work is achieved by taking part in ISO technical committees—the groups that set standards—and by volunteering to coordinate such committees, volunteering to act as their secretariat.

The prominence of global industrial standard setting came, in part, as an indirect consequence of some of ISO's earlier work. In the 1960s and 1970s much of the attention of ISO's own small Geneva-based secretariat, and much of the attention of many national standard setters, was focused on creating standards that would transform the global transportation and communication infrastructure, thus removing a major impediment to the creation of a global trading area. As that global trading area formed, the work of voluntary consensus standard setters shifted more and more toward the establishment of global standards.

At the same time, the recent round of economic globalization confronted companies throughout the world with greater competition as well as greater opportunities for new markets. This provided an incentive for many companies to adopt customer-oriented quality management systems. The ISO 9000 series provided one such system. In fact, it provided the system that has been, by far, the most widely adopted throughout the world.

ISO 9000 proved an economic boon to many national standard setting bodies (and, to a lesser extent, to ISO itself) and led to a strong interest in developing other management systems and other standards for work processes. Developing such standards has become a major focus of ISO's work today. That work includes the now well-established series of ISO environmental standards (ISO 14000) as well as ongoing negotiations on a general standard for corporate social responsibility that will cover issues of labor rights and human rights in general, as well as questions of environmental stewardship, transparency, and support of the rule of law. As ISO has moved into these new fields, it has begun to take on something of that long-anticipated role of setting global social standards—establishing regulations that governments find difficult to establish by themselves or through traditional intergovernmental agreements.

As ISO's role setting standards for quality management, environmental management, and corporate social responsibility have increased, so has the organization's visibility as a part of global governance. Companies advertise their adherence to ISO 9000 and ISO 14000 standards, and, in most countries, consumers have developed some awareness of what that means.

Yet, at the same time that ISO's visibility as part of global governance has increased, the original role of voluntary consensus standard setting has diminished. Throughout the twentieth century, the greatest champions of voluntary consensus standard setting were engineers in the most innovative fields of the day—beginning with electrical engineers a century ago, in the early days of electric power. In today's highest-technology fields, innovation takes place so rapidly that ISO's relatively slow process of building consensus among consumers and producers seems cumbersome and slow to many important stakeholders. Ad hoc consortia of information technology producers have become important standard setters and ISO's goal of serving the public good has been adopted by the open source movement, which is largely made up of engineers in one of today's leading technological fields.

That change has not diminished ISO's role, or that of voluntary consensus standard setting. The organization sits at the center of a network of experts and industry representatives that is as large or larger than the professional staff of the entire United Nations system. The collective work of those standard setters may be as essential to today's global political order as anything done by the UN system. ISO's work is certainly as essential, perhaps more essential, to the governance of the global industrial economy.

Notes

Foreword

1 James Raymond Vreeland, *The International Monetary Fund: Politics of Conditional Lending* (London: Routledge, 2007).
2 Katherine Marshall, *The World Bank: From Reconstruction to Development to Equity* (London: Routledge, 2008).
3 Bernard Hoekman and Petros Mavroidis, *The World Trade Organization: Law, Economics and Politics* (London: Routledge, 2007).
4 Craig N. Murphy, *International Organization and Industrial Change: Global Governance Since 1850* (New York: Oxford University Press, 1994).
5 Craig N. Murphy, *Global Institutions, Marginalization, and Development* (London: Routledge, 2004); Craig N. Murphy and Roger Tooze, *The New International Political Economy* (Boulder, Co.: Lynne Reinner, 1991); Craig N. Murphy, *Egalitarian Politics in an Age of Globalization* (Basingstoke: Palgrave, 2002); Mustapha Kamal Pasha and Craig N. Murphy, *International Relations and the New Inequality* (Oxford: Blackwell, 2002).
6 Craig N. Murphy, *The United Nations Development Programme: A Better Way?* (Cambridge: Cambridge University Press, 2006). Readers can look forward to his forthcoming volume in this series on the UNDP to be co-authored with Elizabeth Mandeville.
7 JoAnne Yates, *Structuring the Information Age: Life Insurance and Information Technology in the 20th Century* (Baltimore, Md.: Johns Hopkins University Press, 2005); JoAnne Yates and John Van Maanen, eds., *IT and Organizational Transformation: History, Rhetoric, and Practice* (London: Sage, 2001); Toshiro Wakayama, Srikanth Kannapan, Chan Meng Khoong, Sham Navathe, and JoAnne Yates, *Proceedings of the International Working Conference on Information and Process Integration in Enterprises* (Norwell, Mass.: Kluwer, 1998); JoAnne Yates, ed., *Control Through Communication: The Rise of System in American Management* (Baltimore, Md.: Johns Hopkins University Press, 1989).

Introduction

1 In 2008, ISO's web page asserted, "Because 'International Organization for Standardization' would have different acronyms in different languages ... its founders decided to give it also a short, all-purpose name. They chose

'ISO', derived from the Greek *isos*, meaning 'equal.'" However, in 1997, the last person living of those who attended ISO's 1946 founding meeting in London said, "I recently read that the name ISO was chosen because 'iso' is a Greek term meaning 'equal.' There was no mention of that in London" Willy Kuert, "The Founding of ISO," in Jack Latimer, compiler, *Friendship Among Equals: Recollections from ISO's First Fifty Years* (Geneva, Switzerland: ISO Central Secretariat, 1997), 20.

2 Paul Gough Agnew, quoted as the epigraph of Dickson Reck, ed., *National Standards in a Modern Economy* (New York: Harper Bros., 1956), v.

3 Sidney and Beatrice Webb, *A Constitution for a Socialist Commonwealth of Great Britain* (London: Longmans, Green and Co., 1920), 56.

4 Alfred Zimmern, "Democracy and the Expert," *The Political Quarterly* 1, no. 1 (1930): 7–25.

5 Harland Cleveland, "Coming Soon: The Nobody-in-Charge Society," *The Futurist* 34, no. 5 (2000): 52–56.

6 J. F. Rischard, *High Noon: Twenty Global Problems: Twenty Years to Solve Them* (New York: Basic Books, 2002).

1 Voluntary consensus standard setting: why it matters and how it arose

1 See JoAnne Yates and Craig N. Murphy, "Coordinating International Standards: The Formation of the ISO," MIT Sloan Research Paper no. 4638–07 (2007), 16.

2 Winton Higgins, *Engine of Change: Standards Australia since 1922* (Blackheath, NSW: Brandl & Schlesinger Book Publishers, 2005), 9.

3 Polly Hill, "Marketplaces," in John Eastwell, Murray Milgate, and Peter Newman, eds., *The New Palgrave: Economic Development* (New York: W. W. Norton & Co., 1989), 238. Polly Hill, "Markets in Africa," *The Journal of Modern African Studies* 1, no. 4 (1963): 441–53.

4 T. C. McCaskie, *State and Society in Pre-Colonial Asante* (Cambridge: Cambridge University Press 1995), 10.

5 Francis Fuller, *A Vanished Dynasty: Ashanti* (London: John Murray, 1921), 28.

6 W. W. Rostow, *The British Economy of the Nineteenth Century* (Oxford: Oxford University Press, 1948), 12–23.

7 Higgins, *Engine of Change*, 9.

8 McCaskie, *State and Society*, 10.

9 Imperialism reflected the "lateral pressure" generated by the modern economy. See Nazli Chourci and Robert C. North, *Nations in Conflict: National Growth and International Violence* (San Francisco, Calif.: W. H. Freeman, 1975).

10 Karl Marx and Friedrich Engels, *Manifesto of the Communist Party* (text from the 1888 English edition, 1848 German original), www.marxists.org/archive/marx/works/1848/communist-manifesto/ch01.htm

11 Paul Gough Agnew, quoted as the epigraph of Dickson Reck, ed., *National Standards in a Modern Economy* (New York: Harper Bros., 1956), v.

12 Albert W. Whitney, "The Place of Standardization in Modern Life," in Richard H. Landsburgh, ed., *Standards in Industry, The Annals of the American Academy of Political and Social Science* 137 (1928): 34.

13 Jean-Daniel Merlet, "Normalisation, réglementation, innovation: dans la construction: opposition ou complémentarité?" in Jean-Pierre Galland, ed.,

"Réglementation, Normalisation, et Innovation," *Annales des Ponts et Chaussées* 95 (2000): 20–27.

14 Hervé Penan, "Normalisation et innovation," in Galland, "Réglementation," 5.

15 Laura Sydell, "Cell Phones Do Double Duty in India," National Public Radio, 24 December 2007, www.npr.org/templates/story/story.php?storyId=17587238

16 Scott Kirsner, "Charging Pads Inching from R&D to Reality," *Boston Globe,* 30 September 2007, www.boston.com/business/technology/articles/2007/09/30/charging_pads_inching_from_rd_to_reality/

17 For example, a former ISO secretary general estimated that 15,000 to 20,000 standards were needed for a highly industrialized society to function. Olle Sturén, "Toward Global Acceptance of International Standards," speech to the National Bureau of Standards in Washington, DC, June 1972, 2. (Papers of Olle Sturén collected by him for a projected memoir.)

18 On the scope of the task that would confront the US Congress if there were no system of voluntary consensus standard setting, see Samuel Krislov, *How Nations Choose Product Standards and Standards Change Nations* (Pittsburgh, Pa.: University of Pittsburgh Press, 1997), 64.

19 "Seigneurage," today, is often defined as the value gained by the political authority that produces a currency in wide use, but the historical root of the word applies to rents gained by any authoritative standard setter.

20 Robert Tavernor, *Smoot's Ear: The Measure of Humanity* (New Haven, Conn.: Yale University Press, 2007), 56, 60.

21 Ibid., 119.

22 Ibid., 131.

23 Ibid., 147.

24 Hendrick Spruyt, "The Supply and Demand of Governance in Standard-Setting: Insights from the Past," *Journal of European Public Policy* 8, no. 3 (2001): 371.

25 Joseph Farrell and Garth Saloner, "Coordination through Committees and Markets," *RAND Journal of Economics* 19, no. 2 (1988): 235–52.

26 "VHS" stands for "Video Home System," "HD DVD" for "High-Definition Digital Video Disc."

27 Thomas A. Loya and John Boli, "Standardization in the World Polity: Technical Rationality over Power," in *Constructing World Culture: International Nongovernmental Organizations since 1875*, eds. John Boli and George M. Thomas (Stanford, Calif.: Stanford University Press, 1999), 176.

28 One of the recent important studies that maintains that usage is the United Kingdom's Department for International Development's controversial assessment of the effectiveness of different multilateral agencies, which distinguishes operational development and humanitarian agencies that provide direct services, such as UNICEF, from the older "standard setting agencies" (e.g., the International Labor Organization and World Health Organization) which also now provide direct services other than the promulgation of standards, their original purpose (Alison Scott, "DFID's Assessment of Multilateral Organisational Effectiveness," International Division Advisory Department, Department for International Development, 1 June 2005, dfid.gov.uk/pubs/files/meff-results.pdf).

29 Craig N. Murphy, *International Organization and Industrial Change: Global Governance since 1850* (New York: Oxford University Press, 1994), 56–62.

30 Mark Frary, "The World of Electricity: 1820–1904," www.iec.ch/about/hist ory/founding_iec.htm.

31 R. E. B. Crompton, *Reminiscences* (London: Constable, 1928), 205; Louis Ruppert, *History of the International Electrotechnical Commission* (Geneva, Switzerland: IEC, 1956), 2.

32 Obituary: "Charles Delacour Le Maistre," *The Journal of the Institution of Electrical Engineers* 101 (1953): 308.

33 Brian Bowers, "Siemens, Alexander (1847–1927)," *Oxford Dictionary of National Biography*, first published 2004, dx.doi.org/10.1093/ref:odnb/48189. "Ichisuke Fujioka: A Wizard with Electricity," www.toshiba.co.jp/spirit/en/ ichisuke/index.html.

34 The quotation is from, "1981 ... A Year of Anniversaries," *IEC Bulletin* 15, no. 67 (1981): 4. The members and minutes of the first meeting are in IEC, "Report of Preliminary Meeting Held at the Hotel Cecil, London, on Tuesday and Wednesday, June 26th and 27th 1906."

35 Larry Randles Lagerstrom, "Constructing Uniformity: The Standardization of International Electromagnetic Measures, 1860–1912," Ph.D. dissertation in History, University of California–Berkeley, 1992, 315.

36 IEC/TC-1, "Strategic Policy Statement," SMB/3395/R, 21 December 2006.

37 Willy Kuert, "The Founding of ISO," in Jack Latimer, compiler, *Friendship Among Equals: Recollections from ISO's First Fifty Years* (Geneva, Switzerland: ISO Central Secretariat, 1997), 16.

38 A chapter subheading in Higgins, *Engine of Change*, 38–43.

39 Ibid., 39.

40 Krislov, *How Nations Choose Product Standards*, 42.

41 See Ellis W. Hawley, "Herbert Hoover, the Commerce Secretariat, and the Vision of an Associative State," *The Journal of American History* 61, no. 1 (1974): 116–40; and on similar developments in Sweden, Hans De Geer, *Rationaliseringsrörelsen i Sverige: effektivitetsidéer och socialt ansvar under mellankrigstide* (Stockholm: Studieförb. Näringsliv o. samhälle [SNS], 1978).

42 JoAnne Yates and Craig N. Murphy, "Charles Le Maistre: Entrepreneur in International Standardization," MIT Sloan Research Paper no. 4652-07 (2007), 17–18.

43 Higgins, *Engine of Change*, 345.

44 C.f. E. H. Carr's classic discussion of the interwar utopians in his *The Twenty Year's Crisis: 1919–1939* (London: Macmillan, 1940). More recent assessments are much more nuanced, e.g. Cecelia Lynch, *Beyond Appeasement: Interpreting Interwar Peace Movements in World Politics* (Ithaca, N.Y.: Cornell University Press, 1999).

45 Translated from Jean-Pierre Galland, "Réglementation, Normalisation, et Innovation," *Annales des Ponts et Chaussées* 95 (2000): 1. Galland works for the French Ministry of Public Works, Transport, and Housing.

46 Mark Nottingham, "So You'd Like to be a Standards Geek," www.amazon. com/gp/richpub/syltguides/fullview/1OL709EFLT7Y0

47 Krislov, *How Nations Choose Product Standards*, 21.

48 Quoted in Robert Coutts McWilliam, "The Evolution of British Standards," Ph.D. dissertation in Management, University of Reading (2002), 248.

49 Perhaps the closest approximation would be a series of articles written in the 1970s by Ian Stewart, the head of the Australian national standards body. See Higgins, *Engine of Change*, 144–46.

50 Kuert, "The Founding of ISO," 18.
51 Roger Maréchal, "The Early Years," in Latimer, *Friendship Among Equals*, 31.
52 Charles Le Maistre, "Standardization: Its Fundamental Importance to the Prosperity of Our Trade," Paper read before the North East Coast Institution of Engineers and Shipbuilders on 24 March 1922 and reprinted by the order of the Council, 1.
53 Higgins, *Engine of Change*, 54–55. Alain Durand, *AFNOR, 80 ans au service de la normalisation* (Paris: AFNOR, 2008), 21–22.
54 Yates and Murphy, "Coordinating International Standards," 19.
55 Quoted from the minutes of the governing board of the US standards body, 10 June 1926, in Yates and Murphy, "Coordinating International Standards," 20.
56 Howard Coonley, "The International Standards Movement," in Dickson Reck, ed., *National Standards in a Modern Economy* (New York: Harper and Brothers, 1956), 38.
57 Ibid., 39.
58 Markus Kuhn, "International Paper Sizes," 16 August 2002, www.a4paper.org. Kuhn, a University of Cambridge computer scientist, is very much part of the standards movement. He writes, "Globalization starts with getting the details right. Inconsistent use of SI units [units agreed upon through ISO and other bodies] and international standard paper sizes remain today a primary cause for US businesses failing to meet the expectations of customers worldwide."
59 See "nano-" on the International System of Units (SI) web site, www.sizes.com/units/nano.htm
60 Quoted from the minutes of the governing board of the US standards body, 10 December 1943, in Yates and Murphy, "Coordinating International Standards," 23.
61 There was a second office in New York. See ibid., 25.
62 "UNSCC," *Economist* 148 (3 March 1945): 286–87.
63 Yates and Murphy, "Coordinating International Standards," 26–37.
64 Many authors have applied this name to these decades. One is Eric Hobsbawm, "The Golden Years," *The Age of Extremes: A History of the World 1914–1991* (New York: Vintage Books, 1996), 257–86.
65 Olle Sturén, "Standardization and Variety Reduction as a Contribution to a Free European Market," in Committee for Scientific Management (CIOS), *Report of the European Management Conference, Berlin* (Geneva, Switzerland: CIOS, 1958), 161.
66 Typescript, "1969," (minutes of a meeting of the ISO council), 12 (Sturén papers).
67 Ibid., 13–14.
68 Ibid., 13.
69 Olle Sturén, "The Expansion of ISO," in Latimer, *Friendship Among Equals*, 62.
70 Typescript, "Statement by the Netherlands Delegation," (n.d., probably November 1964), 1 (Sturén papers).
71 Olle Sturén, speech to the American Society of Mechanical Engineers, New Orleans, La., December 1984, 3–4 (Sturén papers).
72 Olle Sturén, "Responding to the Challenge of the GATT Standards Code," speech to ANSI, Washington, DC, March 1980, 2 (Sturén papers).

73 Ibid., 3.
74 See e.g. Vincent Grey, "1946 ISO—A New Time, A New Start, The Transport Success Story," in *100 Year Commemoration for International Standardization, Addresses Presented, 18 September 1986* (Geneva, Switzerland: ISO, 1986), 46–52.
75 Olle Sturén, "The Scope of ISO," speech to the Standards Council of Canada, Ottawa, Ont., June, 1997, 2–3 (Sturén papers).
76 www.iso.org/iso/home.htm
77 Sturén, typescript, "1969," 14.
78 "About BSI," www.bsiamericas.com/AboutBSIInc/BSIMilestones.xalter
79 Carl F. Cargill, *Open System's Standardization: A Business Approach* (Upper Saddle River, N.J.: Prentice Hall PTR, 1997), 216.

2 How ISO works

1 Especially in the 1970s; for example, the ISO secretary general began a 1972 speech to the US National Bureau of Standards, "ISO, the international Specialized Agency for Standardization" (Olle Sturén, "Toward Global Acceptance of International Standards," Speech to the National Bureau of Standards in Washington, DC, June 1972, 2 (papers of Olle Sturén collected by him for a projected memoir)). The same designation was used at least through 1977, when ISO, with the financial support of UNESCO, published its first major book on information processing standards, with prominent UN system logos and the identification of ISO as the "Specialized Agency for Standardization." ISO, *Information Transfer: Handbook on International Standards Governing Information Transfer*, ISO Standards Handbook no. 1 (Geneva, Switzerland: ISO Information Centre, 1977).
2 "Meet ISO," www.iso.org/iso/about/discover-iso_meet-iso.htm
3 The "WTO TBT Standards Code Directory: Standardizing bodies have accepted the WTO TBT Code of Good Practice for the Preparation, Adoption, and Application of Standards," 31 August 2007, provides information on the 117 of ISO's 158 members who have accepted the code; 76 of the 117 are described as "central government" standardizing bodies, 40 as "non-governmental," and one as mixed.
4 ISO uses a collaborative knowledge management software product, Livelink® that has a variety of applications including a relatively sophisticated system for electronic balloting.
5 Calculated from "Meeting calendar," www.iso.org/iso/standards_development/technical_committees/meeting_calendar.htm
6 "The ISO brand," www.iso.org/iso/about/discover-iso_meet-iso/discover-iso_the-iso-brand.htm
7 "Participation in TCs, Ghana (GSB)," www.iso.org/iso/about/iso_members/iso_member_participation_tc.htm?member_id=1747
8 Throughout ISO's first two decades it was technically only in the business of "coordinating" national standards, not setting new "international" standards. However, its technical committees made "recommendations" that were all but indistinguishable from what were later called "international" or "ISO" standards.
9 "List of ISO technical committees," www.iso.org/iso/standards_development/technical_committees/list_of_iso_technical_committees.htm

10 "Who develops ISO standards," www.iso.org/iso/about/discover-iso_meet-iso/discover-iso_who-develops-iso-standards.htm

11 Olle Sturén, "The Scope of ISO," speech to the Standards Council of Canada, Ottawa, Ont., June 1997, 2–3 (Sturén papers).

12 Harland Cleveland, "Coming Soon: The Nobody-in-Charge Society," *The Futurist* 34, no. 5 (2000): 55.

13 "ISO Standard," www.iso.org/iso/iso_standard_deliverable

14 As was the case in 2007, "TC-114 Horology," www.iso.org/iso/standards_d evelopment/technical_committees/list_of_iso_technical_committees/iso_tech nical_committee.htm?commid=51734; and 30 years ago, Olle Sturén, "The Geography of ISO," speech to the Standards Council of New Zealand, Wellington, March 1977, 3.

15 "The ISO Technical Committees Shown in Figures 1947–64," ISO/GA-1964-8, 14. For Nehru on India and standards see Suresh Jagne and B. S. Kademani, "Standards: Challenges for Collection Development and Organisation," *Indian Journal of Information: Library and Society* 12, no. 2 (1999): 2.

16 Kristina Sandberg, "ISO 26000 – Social Responsibility," paper presented to the ISO working group, Stockholm, 24 February 2006.

17 Craig N. Murphy, *International Organization and Industrial Change: Global Governance since 1850* (New York: Oxford University Press, 1994), 56–62.

18 For the ISO and technical committee estimates see Stanley M. Besen and Garth Saloner, "Compatibility Standards and the Market for Telecommunications Services," in *Changing the Rules: Technological Change, International Competition, and Regulation in Telecommunications*, eds. Robert W. Crandall and Kenneth Flamm (Washington, DC: Brookings Institution Press, 1988), 177–220; and Walter Mattli and Tim Büthe, "Setting International Standards: Technical Rationality or the Primacy of Power?" *World Politics* 56, no. 1 (2003): 7.

19 Mark Nottingham, "So You'd Like to Be a Standards Geek," www.amazon.com/gp/richpub/syltguides/fullview/1OL709EFLT7Y0.

20 Nottingham, "So You'd Like to be a Standards Geek."

21 Olle Sturén, "Collaboration in International Standardization between Industrialized and Developing Countries," speech to the German Institute for Standardization, Bonn, November 1981, 4.

22 "ISO's Structure," www.iso.org/iso/about/structure.htm

23 Ziva Patir, "Demystifying the ISO/TMB," presentation to the ANSI Conference on US Leadership in ISO and the IEC, Phoenix, Ariz., November 2005, 9.

24 This is the view of Sturén's sons, Lars and Lolo, interview with Craig N. Murphy, 20 November 2007. Letters saved by Olle Sturén and written in 1965–68 by H. A. R. Binney, the head of BSI to Sturén and to Vincent Clermont of AFNOR (Sturén papers) would seem to support that view, but they are not conclusive.

25 Olle Sturén, notebook listing travel, 1953–87 (Sturén papers).

26 Lawrence D. Eicher, "Foreword" to Jack Latimer, compiler, *Friendship Among Equals: Recollections from ISO's First Fifty Years* (Geneva, Switzerland: ISO Central Secretariat, 1997), 10.

27 See Chapter 4.

28 Patir, "Demystifying the ISO/TMB," 15.

29 "ISO World Standards Day," www.cira.colostate.edu/cira/RAMM//hillger/standards.htm

30 See, e.g., the five-minute film, "ISO 14001: The World's Environmental Management Standard" (Geneva, Switzerland: ISO, 2007), www.youtube.com/watch?v=uCjK3lQhPDc

31 Roseline Barchietto, "The Work of the Central Secretariat," in Latimer, *Friendship Among Equals*, 89.

32 Carl F. Cargill, *Open System's Standardization: A Business Approach* (Upper Saddle River, N.J.: Prentice Hall PTR, 1997), 204.

33 ISO, "My ISO Job: Guidance for Delegates and Experts," (Geneva, Switzerland: ISO Central Secretariat, 2005), 9.

34 "Organizations in cooperation with ISO," www.iso.org/iso/about/organizations_in_liaison.htm

35 Alan Bryden, Report of the Secretary General, 26th ISO General Assembly, SG/PRD/ID 13237769, 5 September 2003, 19.

36 Randall L. Calvert, "Leadership and Its Basis in Problems of Social Coordination," *International Political Science Review* 13, no. 1 (1992): 9.

37 JoAnne Yates and Craig N. Murphy, "Coordinating International Standards: The Formation of the ISO," MIT Sloan Research Paper no. 4638–07 (2007), 15–17, details some of the debates about this issue within the American Engineering Standards Committee.

38 Ibid.

39 Calvert, "Leadership," 12.

40 Ibid., 14.

41 The book is Cargill, *Open Systems Standardization*.

42 Calvert, "Leadership," 19, would argue that the question is slightly misplaced:

> In an important sense, power is based on leadership. Because the leader produces group benefits ... and because the realization of those benefits requires responsiveness on the part of followers, the leader does indeed have power. But as this model shows, power need not precede leadership at all. Leadership is based on the group's need for solution of social dilemmas; the focalization of the leader confers power.

Nonetheless, the question that we are concerned with at this point is a little different from one Calvert addresses in this paragraph. We are concerned with why members of as technical committee would focus on the solutions offered by particular people on the committee, not on the concern shared by the whole committee to find a solution.

43 It is in this context that historian Andrew Russell calls Cargill a "guru." Andrew Russell, "The American System: A Schumpeterian History of Standardization," *Progress on Point*, Periodic Commentaries on the Policy Debate from the Progress and Freedom Foundation, Release 12 (18 September 2005): 3.

44 E.g. Carl F. Cargill, "Standardization as a Guardian of Innovation," unpublished paper, 27 January 2003.

45 Winton Higgins, *Engine of Change: Standards Australia since 1922* (Blackheath, NSW: Brandl & Schlesinger Book Publishers, 2005), 28–29.

46 Emily Green Balch, "Toward Human Unity or Beyond Nationalism," Nobel Peace Prize Lecture for 1946, nobelprize.org/nobel_prizes/peace/laureates/1946/balch-lecture.html

47 Pierre Bourdieu and Loïc J. D. Wacquant, *An Invitation to Reflexive Sociology* (Chicago: University of Chicago Press, 1992), 119.

48 "ISO in Figures for the Year 2006," www.iso.org/iso/about/iso_in_figures.htm

49 Standards Australia, "Annual Report, 06–07," section 2.

50 BSI, "Annual Review and Summary Financial Statement 2006," 3.

51 Sturén, "The Geography of ISO," 3.

52 In 1977, Sturén cited the estimate of 100,000 (ibid.), which is still widely used.

53 For data on the UN system as a whole see Klaus Hüfner and Michael Renner, "Total UN System Estimated Expenditures," www.globalpolicy.org/finance/tables/system/tabsyst.htm

54 Marc A. Olshan, "Standards Making Organizations and the Rationalization of American Life," *The Sociological Quarterly* 34, no. 2 (1993): 319.

55 Jan Ollner, "Olle Sturén" (Obituary), *Dagens Nyheter*, 3 June 2003, www.dn.se/DNet/jsp/polopoly.jsp?a=157572, cites this as one of Sturén's major accomplishments. Sturén anticipated the significance of this development early in his tenure as secretary general, Sturén, "Toward Global Acceptance," 6–7.

56 OECD, *From Red Tape to Smart Tape: Administrative Simplification in OECD Countries* (Paris: OECD, 2003), 237, 240–41.

57 Olle Sturén, "Developments in International Standardization and their Relevance to Foreign Trade," speech to the Canadian Export Association, October 1981, 2. Sturén was one of the designers of the European standards regime in the late 1950s and early 1960s.

58 ISO and IEC, "WTO, ISO, IEC, and World Trade," www.standardsinfo.net/info/livelink/fetch/2000/148478/6301438/inttrade.html. ISO even treats the WTO's list of all the bodies that conform to the WTO code as one of the seven basic documents that define how ISO's work is governed. See "Governance," www.iso.org/iso/publications_and_e-products/additional_publications/governance.htm#090027

3 Infrastructure for a global market

1 Toby Poston, "Thinking Inside the Box," BBC News, 25 April 2006, news.bbc.co.uk/2/hi/business/4943382.stm

2 See, e.g., Vince Grey, "Setting Standards," in Jack Latimer, compiler, *Friendship Among Equals: Recollections from ISO's First Fifty Years* (Geneva, Switzerland: ISO Central Secretariat, 1997), 33–42 and "Examples of Benefits That Standards Provide," www.iso.org/iso/about/discover-iso_meet-iso/discover-iso_examples-of-the-benefits-standards-provide.htm

3 See ISO, "Metrology, Standardization, and Conformity Assessment: Building an Infrastructure for Sustainable Development," Central Secretariat, February 2006: UN Department of Economic and Social Affairs, 2; Division for Sustainable Development, www.un.org/esa/sustdev/; and "UN Millennium Development Goals," www.un.org/millenniumgoals/

4 To paraphrase the definition of "global governance" offered at the beginning of *Our Global Neighborhood* The Commission on Global Governance (New York: Oxford University Press, 1995), 1.

5 ISO, "Metrology, Standardization, and Conformity Assessment," 2.
6 ISO, "TC-12 Quantities, Units, Symbols, Conversion Factors," www.iso. org/iso/standards_development/technical_committees/list_of_iso_technical_committees/iso_technical_committee.htm?commid=46202
7 ISO, "Metrology, Standardization, and Conformity Assessment," 3.
8 Ibid. IAF, "Certified Once, Accepted Everywhere," IAF, Cherrybrook, NSW, Australia, March 2006, 1.
9 ISO, "TC-96/SC-5 Use, Operation, and Maintenance [of cranes]," www.iso. org/iso/standards_development/technical_committees/list_of_iso_technical_committees/iso_technical_committee.htm?commid=50658
10 ISO, "Metrology, Standardization, and Conformity Assessment," 2.
11 Alan Bryden, "Standardization and Conformity Assessment in Support of Sustainable Development," presentation to the Regional Workshop on Conformity Assessment, Sustainable Development, and Trade, Johannesburg, 9 May 2007, 6.
12 The example is based on Marc Levinson, *The Box: How the Shipping Container Made the World Smaller and the World Economy Bigger* (Princeton, N.J.: Princeton University Press, 2006), 33.
13 See the example in ibid., 9.
14 Poston, "Thinking Inside the Box."
15 David Tinsley, "Containership Design," *Lloyd's List Special Report*, 16 August 2007, www.lloydsshipmanager.com/ll/news/specialReports.htm
16 Hugo van Driel quoted in Tineke M. Egyedi, "The Standardised Container: Gateway Technologies in Cargo Transport," *Homo Oeconomicus* 17, no. 3 (2000): 232.
17 Egyedi, "The Standardised Container," 233.
18 Calculated from Figure 3.6 in Hugo van Driel and Ferry de Goey, *Rotterdam: Cargo Handling Technology, 1870–2000* (Walburg Pers, the Netherlands: Stichting Historie der Techniek, 2000), 95.
19 Poston, "Thinking Inside the Box."
20 Quoted in ibid.
21 Levinson, *The Box*, 189–211. Britain's 1959 economic plan for Singapore imagined that it might someday, in the distant future, develop an economy as large as that of an English county seat, see Craig N. Murphy, *The United Nations Development Programme: A Better Way?* (Cambridge: Cambridge University Press, 2006), 101.
22 Levinson, *The Box*, 204–5.
23 Ibid., 115.
24 William Sjostrom, review of Levinson, *The Box*, eh.net (March 2007) eh. net/bookreviews/library/1205
25 Elizabeth R. DeSombre, *Flagging Standards: Globalization, Environmental, Safety, and Labor Regulation at Sea* (Cambridge, Mass.: MIT Press, 2006) explains why this situation persists at sea. The same argument could apply equally well to conditions in ports since the regulatory control of specific ports is a major part of the explanation of different conditions at sea.
26 Victor Kazanjian, interview with Craig Murphy, 5 February 2007.
27 Poston, "Thinking Inside the Box."
28 Stephen Herzenberg, "In from the Margins: Morality, Economics, and International Labor Rights," in *Human Rights, Labor Rights, and International*

Trade, eds. Lance A. Compa and Stephen D. Diamond (Philadelphia: University of Pennsylvania Press, 1996), 103.

29 Jean-Daniel Merlet, "Normalisation, réglementation, innovation dans la construction: opposition ou complémentarité?" in "Réglementation, Normalisation, et Innovation," ed. Jean-Pierre Galland, *Annales des Ponts et Chaussées* 95 (2000): 20–27.

30 Egyedi, "The Standardised Container," 234.

31 Ibid.

32 Levinson, *The Box*, 30.

33 Vince Grey, "1946 ISO – A New Time, a New Start: The Transport Success Story," in ISO, "100-Year Commemoration for International Standardization, Addresses Presented," Geneva, Switzerland, 18 September 1986, 49.

34 E.g. ibid.; and Grey, "Setting Standards."

35 Grey, "Setting Standards," 30–40.

36 Ibid., 40.

37 Levinson, *The Box*, 130, 132.

38 Ibid., 135–36; Grey, "Setting Standards," 41.

39 Levinson, *The Box*, 133.

40 Ibid., 137.

41 Egyedi, "The Standardised Container," 240.

42 Grey, "Setting Standards," 41.

43 Levinson, *The Box*, 139–40.

44 Grey, "Setting Standards," 41.

45 Ibid.

46 Ibid., 42.

47 Levinson, 143–44.

48 Grey, "Setting Standards," 42.

49 Egyedi, "The Standardised Container," 257.

50 Poston, "Thinking Inside the Box."

51 Egyedi, "The Standardised Container," 257.

52 Ibid., 254–56.

53 Grey quoted in ibid., 247.

54 Grey, "Setting Standards," 42.

55 Winton Higgins, *Engine of Change: Standards Australia since 1922* (Blackheath, NSW: Brandl & Schlesinger Book Publishers, 2005), 28–29.

56 Egyedi, "The Standardised Container," 252.

57 Kwame Nkrumah, *Neo-Colonialism: The Last Stage of Imperialism* (London: Nelson, 1965).

58 Egyedi, "The Standardised Container," 252.

59 Olle Sturén, "The Expansion of ISO," in Latimer, *Friendship Among Equals*, 66. ISO's assistance program for standard setters from the developing world is called the "Robert Oteng Fellowship" in his honor, www.iso.org/iso/about/technical_assistance/features_of_technical_assistance.htm

60 Levinson, *The Box*, 149.

61 Ibid.

62 Egyedi, "The Standardised Container," and Driel and de Goey, *Rotterdam*, provide particularly clear accounts of this process in Europe, where, as in other parts of the world, local authorities played extremely important roles. Levinson, *The Box*, 188–211, gives a global overview.

63 ISO standards, www.iso.org/iso/iso_catalogue.htm

64 Song Yan, "Present Conditions and Prospects for the Development of the Bamboo Plywood Industry in China," in *Beyond Timber: Social, Economic, and Cultural Dimensions of Non-Wood Forest Products in Asia and the Pacific*, eds. Patrick B. Durst and Ann Bishop (Bangkok, Thailand: FAO Regional Office for Asia and the Pacific, 1995), 148.

65 "New Eco-Friendly Containers for CMA CGM," CMA CGM press release, 24 August 2007, www.cma-cgm.com/AboutUs/PressRoom/PressRel easeDetail.aspx?Id=5446

66 ISO, "Freight containers," www.iso.org/iso/iso_cafe_freight_containers.htm. *ISO Standards Handbook: Freight Containers* (Geneva, Switzerland: ISO, 2007).

67 Maarten van de Voort and Kevin A. O'Brien, *"Seacurity"—Improving the Security of the Global Sea-Container Shipping System* (Santa Monica, Calif.: RAND, 2003), 10.

68 Ibid., 1–5.

69 Charles J. Piersall, "A Status Report on ISO Initiatives to Enhance Supply Chain Security," presentation to the International Conference on Standardization and Quality, Tel Aviv, Israel, 31 May 2005.

70 David Taylor, "Introduction: 100 Years of Raising Standards," in Robert C. McWilliam, *BSI: The First Hundred Years 1901–2001* (London: Thanet Press, 2001), 6.

71 Inspectorate, "About Us," www.inspectorate.com/about_us/history.asp

72 Container inspection became a major topic in the 2004 US presidential debates, with the Democratic Party candidate arguing that only 5 percent of the containers coming to the United States were inspected beforehand. While it is true that US officials inspect only 5 percent of containers, those whose cargo is considered "high-risk," the selection of what is "high-risk" is based on what is written on manifests that Inspectorate and its competitors have verified as corresponding to what is in the container. CBS News, "Fact Check on the Final Debate," 13 October 2004, www.cbsnews.com/stories/2004/10/13/politics/main649217.shtml

73 Sidney and Beatrice Webb, *A Constitution for a Socialist Commonwealth of Great Britain* (London: Longmans, Green and Co., 1920), 56.

74 These are two of the 1,062 standards in a search for "testing" in the ISO catalogue, www.iso.org/iso/iso_catalogue.htm

75 ISO, "CASCO: Committee on Conformity Assessment," www.iso.org/iso/iso_catalogue/catalogue_tc/catalogue_tc_browse.htm?commid=54998

76 "ANB Background," www.anab.org/

77 Higgins, *Engine of Change*, 216–19.

78 "IAF Members," www.iaf.nu/

79 Higgins, *Engine of Change*, 178.

80 BSI, "History of BSI Group," www.bsi-global.com/en/About-BSI/About-BSI-Group/BSI-History/

81 "About IAF," www.iaf.nu/

82 Adam Smith, *An Inquiry into the Nature and Causes of the Wealth of Nations* (London: printed for W. Strahan and T. Cadell, 1776), book 1, chapter 10.

4 From quality management to social regulation

1 Winton Higgins, *Engine of Change: Standards Australia since 1922* (Blackheath, NSW: Brandl & Schlesinger Book Publishers, 2005), 28.

2 Michael J. Piore, "Labor Standards and Business Strategies," in *Labor Strategies in the Global Economy*, eds. Stephen A. Herzenberg and Jorge F. Pérez-López (Washington, DC: US Department of Labor, Bureau of International Affairs, 1990), 35–49.

3 Stephen Herzenberg, "In From the Margins: Morality, Economics, and International Labor Rights," in *Human Rights, Labor Rights, and International Trade*, eds. Lance A. Compa and Stephen D. Diamond (Philadelphia: University of Pennsylvania Press, 1996), 99–117.

4 Matthew Potoski and Aseem Prakash, "Information Asymmetries as Trade Barriers: ISO 9000 Increases International Commerce," unpublished paper, University of Washington, Department of Political Science, 15 January 2008, 2.

5 Khalid Nadvi and Frank Wältring, "Making Sense of Global Standards," Institut für Entwicklung und Frieden der Gerhard-Mercator-Universität Duisburg, Heft 58, 2002, 34.

6 *The ISO Survey—2005* (Geneva, Switzerland: ISO Central Secretariat, 2006), 8.

7 Denise Robitaille, "ISO 9000: Then and Now," *Quality Digest* 25, no. 11 (2006): 27. It has become common for humanitarian relief organizations to adopt the standard for reasons outlined by Medair's operations director, David Verboom. "The ISO 9001 Quality Approach: Useful for the Humanitarian Aid Sector?" *ReliefWeb*, 23 January 2002, www.reliefweb. int/rw/rwb.nsf/AllDocsByUNID/25f9cf5a7c0b4ab0c1256b4b00367719

8 Hutchins was quoting Thorstein Veblen. John Sayle Watterson, *College Football: History, Spectacle, Controversy* (Baltimore, Md.: Johns Hopkins University Press, 2000), 195.

9 Deming quoted in David E. Genevay, "Stepping through an ISO 9000 Process and Its Myths," *Journal for Quality and Participation* 20, no. 1 (1997): 81. Evidence of the importance of signaling in the adoption of ISO 9000 can be found in a 60-nation study, Xun Cao and Aseem Prakash, "Signaling Quality: Trade Competition and the Cross-Country Diffusion of ISO 9000–Quality Management Systems," unpublished paper, University of Washington, Department of Political Science, 8 February 2008. There is also some evidence that ultimate consumers, at least in Great Britain, see ISO 9000 certification as a guarantee of quality. A 2006 Nottingham University Business School survey found this especially true among "males, in higher income groups, in higher-status social grades, and ages 35–54," ISO press release, "Do Consumers Really Care About ISO 9001:2000 Certification?" 8 June 2006, www.iso.org/iso/pressrelease.htm?refid=Ref1014

10 In early 2008, the three standards were ISO 9000–QMS–Fundamentals and vocabulary, ISO 9001–QMS–Requirements, and ISO 9004–QMS–Guidelines for performance improvements.

11 John Seddon, *The Case Against ISO 9000*, 2nd ed. (Dublin, Ireland: Oak Tree Press, 2000), 142–43.

12 JoAnne Yates, *Control through Communication: The Rise of System in American Management* (Baltimore, Md.: Johns Hopkins University Press, 1989), 264–69.

13 William M. Tsutsui, *Manufacturing Ideology: Scientific Management in Twentieth-Century Japan* (Princeton, N.J.: Princeton University Press, 2001), 197–201.

14 Seddon, *The Case Against ISO 9000*, 1.
15 Lars and Lolo Sturén, interview with Craig N. Murphy, 20 November 2007; Kristina Tamm Hallström, *Organizing International Standardization: ISO and the IASC in Quest of Authority* (Cheltenham: Edward Elgar, 2004), 53–54.
16 Carl F. Cargill, *Open Systems Standardization: A Business Approach* (Upper Saddle River, N.J.: Prentice Hall PTR, 1997), 216.
17 Higgins, *Engine of Change*, 212.
18 Staffan Furusten, "The Knowledge Base of Standards," in Nils Brunsson, Bengt Jacobsson, and associates, *A World of Standards* (Oxford: Oxford University Press, 2000), 72–84.
19 Cargill, *Open Systems Standardization*, 204.
20 Robert Lundquist, "Quality Systems and ISO 9000 in Higher Education," *Assessment and Evaluation in Higher Education* 22, no. 2 (1997): 161.
21 Quoted in R. Dan Reid, "Going Beyond ISO 9001, QS-9000, and TS 16949," *Quality Progress* 35, no. 8 (2002): 81.
22 Cornelia Stortz, "Compliance with International Standards: the EDIFACT and ISO 9000 Standards in Japan," *Social Science Japan Journal* 10, no. 2 (2007): 230; Furusten, "The Knowledge Base of Standards."
23 Tanu Agrawal, "Fear and Desire in Systems Design: Negotiating Database Usefulness," Ph.D. dissertation in Management, Massachusetts Institute of Technology, 2008, 190.
24 Cargill, *Open Systems Standardization*, 204.
25 See Seddon, *The Case Against ISO 9000*, 161–78 for the more muted criticism of the 2000 version of the standard and Takaji Nishizawa's "Eight Principles for ISO 9000 Implementation," in the same volume, 179–81.
26 Lawrence D. Eicher, "International Standardization: Live or Let Die," keynote address to the Canadian Forum on International Standardization, 17 November 1999, 6.
27 R. Dan Reid, "Why QS-9000 Was Developed and What's in Its Future," *Quality Progress* 33, no. 4 (2000): 115.
28 *The ISO Survey—2005*, 10.
29 Lundquist, "Quality Systems and ISO 9000 in Higher Education," 166.
30 Stortz, "Compliance with International Standards," 29.
31 Ibid., 29–30.
32 Isin Guler, Mauro F. Guillén, and John Muir Macpherson, "Global Competition, Institutions, and the Diffusion of Organizational Practices: The International Spread of ISO 9000 Quality Certificates," *Administrative Science Quarterly* 47, no. 2 (2002): 207–32.
33 Ibid.; Genevay, "Stepping through an ISO 9000 Process."
34 Eric Neumayer and Richard Perkins, "Uneven Geographies of Organizational Practice: Explaining the Cross-National Transfer and Diffusion of ISO 9000," *Economic Geography* 81, no. 3 (2005): 237–60.
35 Nadvi and Wältring, "Making Sense of Global Standards," 4.
36 Stortz, "Compliance with International Standards," 20.
37 *The ISO Survey—2005*, 10.
38 Recall Chapter 1, page 10.
39 ISO, "Origins and ISO/TC 207," www.iso.org/iso/iso_catalogue/management_standards/iso_9000_iso_14000/origins_and_iso_tc207.htm

40 Kevin Hershey, " A Close Look at ISO 14000," *Professional Safety* 43, no. 7 (1998): 26–29.
41 Aseem Prakash and Matthew Potoski, *The Voluntary Environmentalists: Green Clubs, ISO 14001, and Voluntary Environmental Regulation* (Cambridge: Cambridge University Press), 146–71.
42 Aseem Prakash and Matthew Potoski, "Racing to the Bottom? Trade, Environmental Governance, and ISO 14001," *American Journal of Political Science* 50, no. 2 (2006): 350–64.
43 E.g. Paul Langley, "Transparency in the Making of Global Environmental Governance," *Global Society* 15, no. 1 (2001): 73–92.
44 Prakash and Potoski, *The Voluntary Environmentalist*, 111.
45 Based on this perspective, they suggest how the rules of voluntary regulatory structures should be set to assure the highest level of compliance, Aseem Prakash and Matthew Potoski, "Collective Action through Voluntary Consensus: A Club Theory Perspective," *Policy Studies Journal* 25, no. 4 (2007): 773–92.
46 "ISO 14001: The World's Environmental Management Standard" (Geneva, Switzerland: ISO, 2007), www.youtube.com/watch?v=uCjK3lQhPDc
47 Quoted in Suzanne Shanahan and Sanjeev Khagram, "Dynamics of Corporate Responsibility," in *Globalization and Organization: World Society and Organizational Change*, eds. Gili S. Drori, John M. Meyer, and Hokyu Wang (Oxford: Oxford University Press, 2006), 198.
48 Ibid., 207.
49 Jennifer Clapp, "The Privatization of Global Environmental Governance: ISO 14000 and the Developing World," *Global Governance* 4, no. 3 (1998): 303, 307.
50 Ibid., 310.
51 Craig N. Murphy, *The United Nations Development Programme: A Better Way?* (Cambridge: Cambridge University Press, 2006), 177–81, 274–75.
52 Zhou Xin, "China Orders Listed Firms to Be Greener," *Reuters*, 25 February 2008, www.reuters.com/article/environmentNews/idUSPEK13520 080225
53 Shanahan and Khagram, in "Dynamics of Corporate Responsibility," look in detail at Brazil and South Africa and present supporting data on India and Thailand.
54 These included UNDP as well as the UN Environmental Programme. In Brazil, UNDP helped the new democratic government circumvent an entrenched alliance between the military and powerful, protected industries that controlled key ministries. Many important parts of the government became (and still are) "UNDP projects," which allowed the new democratic leaders to displace entrenched civil servants in parts of the state structure that would not respond to the new policy directives. See Murphy, *The United Nations Development Programme*, 211–20.
55 Ricardo Young, "Dilemmas and Advances in Corporate Social Responsibility in Brazil: The Work of the Ethos Institute," *Natural Resources Forum* 28, no. 4 (2004): 292. Young heads the Ethos Institute, a trade association of more than 800 companies with aggregate revenues equal to about one-third of Brazil's GDP.
56 Ibid.; Shanahan and Khagram, "Dynamics of Corporate Responsibility," 203, 222.

57 Shanahan and Khagram, "Dynamics of Corporate Responsibility," 215–21. It is not necessarily the case that bankers who have been forced to take on such a role will react by embracing corporate responsibility. Shanahan and Khagram, p. 223, point to the critically important role, in Brazil, of an individual, Amador Aguiar, founder of Brazil's largest private bank, Bradesco: "Part of the story must be Aquiar [sic] whose Catholic childhood as part of Brazil's underclass led him to understand a human being's personal (moral) commitments in a particular way—a way that Bradesco's profitability, international activists, and the UN each supported." Other scholars note that while Bradesco was long at the forefront of the movement for social responsibility, its actions have not necessarily kept up the rapid developments of the last decade: Elvira Cruvinel Ferreira Ventura, and Marcelo Milano Falcao Vieira, "Social Responsibility as Displacement of Capitalism: Evidences from Banks in Brazil," *Electronic Journal of Business and Organization Studies* 12, no. 1 (2007): 35–47.

58 In Marx and Engels's words, see page 7.

59 Woodrow Wilson, *Division and Reunion, 1829–1889* (New York: Longmans, Green, 1893).

60 Craig N. Murphy, "Private Sector," in *The Oxford Handbook on the United Nations*, eds. Thomas G. Weiss and Sam Daws (Oxford: Oxford University Press, 2007), 268–70.

61 Nadvi and Wältring, "Making Sense of Global Standards," 27.

62 Catia Gregoratti, "The UN Global Compact as a Neutral Broker?" Paper presented at the annual meeting of the Academic Council on the UN System, New York, June 2007, 1.

63 Social Accountability International, www.sa8000.org

64 Kristina Tamm Hallström, "International Standardization Backstage: Legitimacy and Competition in the Social Responsibility Field." Paper presented at the conference on Organizing the World—Rules and Rule-Setting Among Organizations, Stockholm Centre for Organizational Research, October 2005, 7.

65 Kristina Sandberg (secretary of the ISO 26000 secretariat) interview with Maria Nassén, 16 January 2008.

66 Tamm Hallström, "International Standardization Backstage," 8–9, 14.

67 The TMB asked North–South pairs of member bodies to volunteer for the secretariat. Two other groups—one involving Germany, the other Japan—also volunteered. Sandberg interview.

68 SIS, "Vägledning för Socialt ansvarstagande ISO 26000," January 2007, 27, 28; "Ethos—ISO 26000," www.ethos.org.br/DesktopDefault.aspx?TabID=4211&Alias=Ethos&Lang=pt-BR

69 Tamm Hallström, "International Standardization Backstage," 24.

70 Sandberg interview. The various electronic discussions are linked through iso.org/wgsr. The protests at the 2006 meeting are discussed in Kristina Tamm Hallström, "ISO Expands Its Business into Social Responsibility," in *Organizing Transnational Accountability*, eds. Magnus Boström and Christina Garsten (Cheltenham: Edward Elgar, 2008), forthcoming.

71 Ibid.

72 Ibid.

73 Tamm Hallström, "International Standardization Backstage," 24.

74 John Gerard Ruggie, "Business and Human Rights: The Evolving International Agenda," *The American Journal of International Law* 101, no. 4 (2007): 830–32.

75 Ralph Hamann, Tagbo Agbazue, Paul Kapelus, and Anders Hein, "Universalizing Corporate Social Responsibility? South African Challenges to the International Organization for Standardization's New Social Responsibility Standard," *Business and Society Review* 101, no.1 (2005): 1–19.

76 This problem is not new. Robert W. Cox pointed out that the same divide existed almost 150 years ago when the first proponents of "international labor legislation" were interested in protecting high-wage jobs in the first European countries that had industrialized from the pressure of the lower wages prevalent in countries on their immediate periphery. Labor "solidarity" was not particularly evident in that movement, Robert W. Cox, "The Idea of International Labor Regulation," in Cox with Timothy J. Sinclair, *Approaches to World Order* (Cambridge: Cambridge University Press, 2001): 41–49. Similarly, while there are some contemporary examples of North–South alliances to promote higher labor standards, they are relatively unusual. See Christopher Candland, "How are International Labor Standards Advanced?" Paper presented to the Council on Foreign Relations, New York, 29 October 2004.

77 Peter Utting, "CSR and Equality," *Third World Quarterly* 28, no. 4 (2007): 700–1.

78 Michael J. Watts, "Righteous Oil? Human Rights, the Oil Complex, and Corporate Social Responsibility," *Annual Review of Environment and Resources* 30, no. 1 (2005): 390.

79 Sandberg interview.

80 Nalle Sturén, interview with Maria Nassén, 13 January 2008.

5 Standards wars and the future of ISO

1 Carl F. Cargill, *Open Systems Standardization: A Business Approach* (Upper Saddle River, N.J.: Prentice Hall PTR, 1997), 301.

2 Walter Mattli and Tim Büthe, "Setting International Standards: Technical Rationality or the Primacy of Power?" *World Politics* 56, no. 1 (2003): 1–42.

3 Mark Schapiro, "New Power for 'Old Europe,'" *International Journal of Health Services* 35, no. 3 (2005): 551–60.

4 "Neo-neo" is a common way to refer to both the similarities between the two theories and to their differences. See, e.g., Heikki Patomäki and Colin Wight, "After Postpositivism? The Promises of Critical Realism," *International Studies Quarterly* 44, no. 2 (2000): 213–37.

5 Mattli and Büthe, "Setting International Standards." Contrast their position to that of Thomas A. Loya and John Boli, "Standardization in the World Polity: Technical Rationality over Power," in *Constructing World Culture: International Nongovernmental Organizations since 1875*, eds. John M. Boli and George M. Thomas (Stanford, Calif.: Stanford University Press, 1999), 169–97.

6 Stephen D. Krasner, "Global Communications and National Power: Life on the Pareto Frontier," *World Politics* 43, no. 3 (1991): 336–66.

7 See Neil Fligstein, "The Political and Economic Sociology of International Economic Arrangements," in *The Handbook of Economic Sociology*, 2nd

ed., eds. Neil J. Smelser and Richard Swedberg (Princeton, N.J.: Princeton University Press, 2005), 183–204.

8 Mattli and Büthe, "Setting International Standards," 23–24. Compare pages 11 and 29.

9 Ibid., 27.

10 Carl F. Cargill and Sherrie Bolin, "Standardization: A Failing Paradigm," in *Standards and Public Policy*, eds. Shane Greenstein and Victor Stango (Cambridge: Cambridge University Press, 2007), 321–22.

11 Jean-Pierre Galland, "Normalisation, construction de l'Europe et mondialisation elements de réflexion," *Notes du Centre de Prospective et de Veille Scientifique* 14 (March 2001): 38.

12 Paul Krugman, "America Loses the Wireless Race—Again," 30 November 2007, krugman.blogs.nytimes.com/2007/11/30/america-loses-the-wireless-rac e-again/. Krugman quotes the *Financial Times*'s chief business commentator, John Gapper.

13 See Cathie Jo Martin, "Sectional Parties, Divided Business," *Studies in American Political Development* 20, no. 2 (2006): 160–84; and Cathie Jo Martin and Duane Swank, "The Political Origins of Coordinated Capitalism: Business Organizations, Party Systems, and State Structures in the Age of Innocence," *American Political Science Review*, forthcoming. Jan Ollner, "Olle Sturén," (Obituary) *Dagens Nyheter,* 3 June 2003, www. dn.se/DNet/jsp/polopoly.jsp?a=157572.

14 After investigating the events that bother so many US firms and scholars publishing in US journals, Olivier Borraz, a sociologist at the French Centre National de la Recherche Scientifique, concludes that the history makes "a case for unintentionality in policy instruments." Olivier Borraz, "Governing Standards: The Rise of Standardization Processes in France and the EU," *Governance* 20, no. 1 (2007): 57.

15 Olle Sturén, "Developments in International Standardization and their Relevance to Foreign Trade," speech to the Canadian Export Association, October 1981 (papers of Olle Sturén collected by him for a projected memoir).

16 Hans W. Micklitz, "Review of Rüdiger Rönck, *Technische Normen als Gesaltungsmittel des Europäischen Gemeinschaftsrechts: Zulässigkeit und Praktikabilität ihrer Rezeption zur Realisierung des gemeinsamen Marktes* (Berlin, Germany: Duncker & Humblot, 1995)," *European Journal of International Law* 9, no. 3 (1998): 574.

17 Galland, "Normalisation, construction de l'Europe et mondialisation," 9.

18 Marine Moguen-Toursel, "European Standards—Tool or Barrier for European Enterprise?" Paper presented at the XIVth International Economic History Congress, Helsinki, Finland, August 2006.

19 See pages 43–4.

20 Tineke Egyedi, *Shaping Standardization: A Study of Standards Processes and Standards Policies in the Field of Telematic Services* (Delft, the Netherlands: Delft University Press, 1996), 125; Galland, "Normalisation, construction de l'Europe et mondialisation," 10.

21 Egyedi, *Shaping Standardization*, 148.

22 Joseph Farrell and Garth Saloner, "Coordination through Committees and Markets," *RAND Journal of Economics* 19, no. 2 (1988): 235–52.

23 Cargill and Bolin, "Standardization," 322.

24 US Department of Commerce, "Roundtable on Transatlantic Standards Issues: Meeting Notes," Washington, DC, 10 January 2005, www.state.gov/p/eur/rls/or/41958.htm
25 Ibid.
26 Benjamin J. Cohen, *International Political Economy: An Intellectual History* (Princeton, N.J.: Princeton University Press, 2008), 66–94.
27 Robert Paarlberg, *Starved for Science: How Biotechnology is Being Kept Out of Africa* (Cambridge, Mass.: Harvard University Press, 2008).
28 Galland, "Normalisation, construction de l'Europe et mondialisation," 15.
29 Illka Toumi, "The Lives and Death of Moore's Law," *First Monday* 7, no. 11 (2002), www.firstmonday.org/issues/issue7_11/tuomi/
30 Egyedi, *Shaping Standardization*, 108.
31 Ibid., 118, quoting a joint ISO/IEC policy document.
32 Andrew L. Russell, "Telecommunication Standards in the Second and Third Industrial Revolutions," *The Journal of Communications Networks* 5, no. 1 (2006): 104.
33 Herbert Bertine, Igor Faynberg, and Hui-Lan Lu, "Overview of Data and Telecommunications Security Standardization Efforts in ISO, IEC, and IETF," *Bell Labs Technical Journal* 8, no. 4 (2004): 206.
34 Quoted in Russell, "Telecommunication Standards," 104; and see Andrew L. Russell, "'Rough Consensus and Running Code' and the Internet–OSI Standards War," *IEEE Annals of the History of Computing* 28, no. 3 (2006): 48–61.
35 Russell, "Telecommunication Standards," 104.
36 Ibid.
37 Some sense of the conflict between "bureaucratic" standard setters and the anarchistic engineers can be gained from a detailed study of the standard setting discussions among the main developers and users of the primary artificial intelligence language, Lisp. These discussions were triggered by the insistence of the major funder of that experimental work, the US Department of Defense. See JoAnne Yates and Wanda J. Orlikowski, "Knee-jerk Anti-LOOPism and other E-mail Phenomena: Oral, Written, and Electronic Patterns in Computer-Mediated Communication," MIT Center for Coordination Science Working Paper no. 150, July, 1993; and Wanda J. Orlikowski and JoAnne Yates, "Genre Repertoire: The Structuring of Communicative Practices in Organizations," *Administrative Science Quarterly* 39, no. 4 (1994): 541–74.
38 James Surowiecki, "Standard-Bearers," *New Yorker*, 16 October 2006, 66.
39 Egyedi, *Shaping Standardization*, 112; Richard Hawkins, "Vers une évolution ou vers une disparition de la 'démocratie technique'? L'avenir de la normalisation dans le domaine des technologies de l'information et de la communication," *Réseaux* 18, no. 102 (2000): 123.
40 Lori Rosenkopf, Anca Metiu, and Varghese P. George, "From Bottom Up? Technical Committee Activity and Alliance Formation," *Administrative Science Quarterly* 46, no. 4 (2001): 748–72. The quotation is from page 748.
41 Cargill and Bolin, "Standardization," 328.
42 Bertine, Faynberg, and Lu, "Overview," 203.
43 "The Tao of IETF: A Novice's Guide to the Internet Engineering Task Force," www.ietf.org/tao.html
44 Bertine, Faynberg, and Lu, "Overview," 206.

45 Bob Sutor, "Striking the Right Chord, If You Can Find It," www.sutor. com/newsite/cv.php. One of the most widely accepted definitions of "open source" is that of the Open Source Initiative, opensource.org/docs/osd

46 Sturén called OSI "one of the big achievements" of ISO during his tenure. Olle Sturén, "Information Management: The Standards Contribution," speech to the International Information Management Conference, Amsterdam, October 1985 (Sturén papers).

47 Cargill, *Open Systems Standardization*, 73–74.

48 Ibid., 74.

49 "'Rough Consensus and Running Code,'" 55. "TCP/IP" stands for "Transmission Control Protocol/Internet Protocol.

50 Cargill and Bolin, "Standardization," 328.

51 Cargill, *Open Systems Standardization*, 280–82.

52 Hawkins, "Vers une évolution," 132.

53 Tineke M. Egyedi, "Why Java™ Was *Not* Standardized Twice," *Computer Standards and Interfaces* 23, no. 4 (2001): 253–65.

54 Raghu Garud, Sanjay Jain, and Arun Kumaraswamy, "Institutional Entrepreneurship in the Sponsorship of Common Technological Standards: The Case of Sun Microsystems and Java," *Academy of Management Journal* 45, no.1 (2002): 209.

55 One of the first declarations of the open source community as a social movement was made by Eric S. Raymond, *The Cathedral and the Bazaar: Musings on Linux and Open Source by an Accidental Revolutionary* (Sebastopol, Calif.: O'Reilly and Associates, 1999), xii.

56 Steven Weber, *The Success of Open Source* (Cambridge, Mass.: Harvard University Press, 2004), 116.

57 Russell, "Telecommunication Standards," 104.

58 Cargill and Bolin, "Standardization," 328.

59 Tineke M. Egyedi and Ruben van Wendel de Joode, "Standardization and Other Coordination Mechanisms in Open Source Software," *Journal of IT Standards and Standardization Research* 2, no. 2 (2004): 1–17.

60 See, Egyedi, *Shaping Standardization*, 118; Russell, "Telecommunication Standards," 104.

61 Timothy S. Simcoe and Marc Rysman, "Measuring the Performance of Standard-Setting Organizations," in *International Standardization as a Strategic Tool* (Geneva, Switzerland: IEC, 2006), 81–93.

Select bibliography

Books

Aseem Prakash and Matthew Potoski, *The Voluntary Environmentalists: Green Clubs, ISO 14001, and Voluntary Environmental Regulations* (Cambridge: Cambridge University Press, 2006). Prakash and Potoski provide a theoretically grounded empirical study of the adoption and impact of ISO's first major attempt at global governance in a field far removed from the technical fields for which the voluntary consensus standard setting process was originally developed.

Carl F. Cargill, *Open Systems Standardization: A Business Approach* (Upper Saddle River, N.J.: Prentice Hall PTR, 1997). Cargill develops a theory of industrial standardization, provides a lucid introduction to consensus standard setting and to the institutions involved and the ways they work. His analysis helps us see the similarities between traditional voluntary consensus standard setting and the current "Open Systems" and "Open Source" movements.

Jack Latimer, compiler, *Friendship Among Equals: Recollections from ISO's First Fifty Years* (Geneva, Switzerland: ISO Central Secretariat, 1997). ISO's official history written for its 50th anniversary consists of eight essays by leading officials and long-term members of the staff. The essays are quasi-chronologically organized and are surprisingly insightful for what was largely meant to be a celebratory volume.

Robert Tavernor, *Smoot's Ear: The Measure of Humanity* (New Haven, Conn.: Yale University Press, 2007). The author is an architect and a professor of urban design. He is critical of the scientism of the modern movement to establish universally applicable, abstract, measures of fundamental units of length, weight, time, etc. He reports a great deal about the history of standard setting that does not appear in the accounts written by those who are part of the standards movement. His discussion of the reluctance and ineffectiveness of most government standard setters is especially interesting.

Web sites

ISO: www.iso.org/iso/home.htm (This well organized web site is primarily aimed at the users of ISO standards. The "ISO Café," www.iso.org/iso/

theisocafe.htm, is a good starting point for social scientists and students interested in investigating the impact of international standards in particular fields.)

IEC: www.iec.ch/ (For students of fields in which the International Electrotechnical Commission has been involved, the IEC web site is even richer than ISO's. The 100th anniversary of the organization, in 2006, led to the development of a particularly rich set of resources including original documents that have been scanned and uploaded and a series of films covering the development of the commission's work, www.iec.ch/about/history/)

ISO/IEC Information Centre: www.standardsinfo.net/info/livelink/fetch/2000/148478/6301438/index.html (This site is jointly maintained by the linked organizations. The "Inventory of Studies on the Economic and Social Benefits of Standardization," www.standardsinfo.net/info/livelink/fetch/2000/148478/6301438/benefits/benefits.html, is especially useful, but it gives priority "to items of general interest and broad impact, and to those freely available on the World Wide Web" and, therefore, cannot be relied upon for a complete bibliography on any topic. Nonetheless, it is surprisingly rich, and well worth consulting when trying to assess the impact of standard setting in any field.)

ITU-T: www.itu.int/ITU-T/index.html (The International Telecommunications Union is the third of the major bodies setting international standards in telecommunications and information technology.)

Some major regional and national standard-setting bodies (in English when available)

Australia SA: www.standards.org.au/
Brazil ABNT: www.abnt.org.br/default.asp?resolucao=1440X900 (in Portuguese)
Canada SCC: www.scc.ca/
China SAC: www.sac.gov.cn/templet/english/
Europe CEN: www.cen.eu/cenorm/homepage.htm
France AFNOR: www.afnor.fr/portail.asp?Lang=English
Germany DIN: www.din.de/cmd?level=tpl-home&languageid=en
India BIS: www.bis.org.in/
Japan JISC: www.jisc.go.jp/eng/index.html
Korea, Rep. of KSA: www.ksa.or.kr/eng/
Netherlands NEN: www2.nen.nl/nen/servlet/dispatcher.Dispatcher?id=ABOUT_NEN
Russia GOSTR: www.gost.ru/wps/portal/ (in Russian)
Sweden SIS: www.sis.se/DefaultMain.aspx
UK BSI: www.bsi-global.com/
USA ANSI: www.ansi.org/

Index

GLOBAL INSTITUTIONS SERIES

NEW TITLE
Institutions of the Global South

Jacqueline Anne Braveboy-Wagner, City University of New York, USA

This is an accessible new introduction to organizations of key importance to the global south in the post-war period. It clearly assesses their achievements, performance and responses to global change.

Selected contents: Introduction 1 Tricontinental diplomacy
2 Tricontinental functionalism 3 Tricontinental single-issue functionalism
4 Regional visions: Pan-Americanism 5 Regional visions: Pan-Africanism
6 Regional visions: Pan-Arabism and Pan-Islam 7 Subregional communities: Latin America and the Caribbean 8 Subregional communities: Africa 9 Subregional communities: Southeast, South, and West Asia, and the Pacific 10 Summarizing global south institutionalism

September 2008: 216x138: 272pp
Hb: 978-0-415-36590-1: **£65.00**
Pb: 978-0-415-36591-8: **£14.99**

NEW TITLE
International Judicial Institutions
The architecture of international justice at home and abroad

Richard J. Goldstone and
Adam M. Smith

Written by a former UN Chief Prosecutor and a leading international law expert, this book is a much needed, short and accessible introduction to the current debates in international humanitarian law and the history and development of strategies and institutions responsible for implementing international justice.

Selected contents: Introduction 1 International humanitarian law: a short review 2 The pre-dawn of international justice: through World War I 3 International justice following World War II: Nuremberg and Tokyo
4 The Cold War and the rise of domestic international justice 5 Post-Cold War justice: the UN ad hoc tribunals, mixed courts, and the ICC
6 Post-ICC prosecutions: new domestic proceedings and international proceedings beyond ICC justice 7 Conclusion: the future of "international" justice—active at home and abroad

September 2008: 216x138: 192pp
Hb: 978-0-415-77645-5: **£65.00**
Pb: 978-0-415-77646-2: **£16.99**

Routledge
Taylor & Francis Group

To order any of these titles
Call: +44 (0) 1235 400400
Email: book.orders@routledge.co.uk

For further information visit:
www.routledge.com/politics

GLOBAL INSTITUTIONS SERIES

NEW TITLE
Global Food and Agricultural Institutions

D. John Shaw

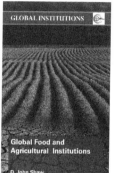

This book examines the origins, functioning and work, successes and difficulties, and the continuing relevance of four UN bodies to meet the challenges of the 21st century.

Selected contents: 1. Background 2. Origins 3. Mandate, governance and finance 4. Policies, programs and projects 5. Future Directions

November 2008: 216x138: 272pp
Hb: 978-0-415-44503-0: **£85.00**
Pb: 978-0-415-44504-7: **£17.99**

NEW TITLE
Shaping the Humanitarian World

Peter Walker, Tufts University and
Daniel Maxwell, Tufts University

This book provides a critical introduction to the notion of humanitarianism in global politics, tracing the concept from its origins to the twenty-first century.

Selected contents: 1. Origins of the international humanitarian system 2. Mercy and manipulation in the Cold War 3. The Globalization of humanitarianism: from the end of the Cold War to the global war on terror 4. States as responders and donors 5. International organizations 6. NGOs and private action 7. Our brave new world, a better future?

November 2008: 216x138: 192pp
Hb: 978-0-415-77370-6: **£65.00**
Pb: 978-0-415-77371-3: **£14.99**

Routledge
Taylor & Francis Group

To order any of these titles
Call: +44 (0) 1235 400400
Email: book.orders@routledge.co.uk

For further information visit:
www.routledge.com/politics

Printed in Great Britain
by Amazon